WORDLY WISE 3000®

Book 6

SECOND EDITION

Kenneth Hodkinson | Sandra Adams

EDUCATORS PUBLISHING SERVICE
Cambridge and Toronto

Original cover design: Hugh Price
Interior design: Sarah Cole
Acquisitions/Development: Kate Moltz
Editors: Wendy Drexler, Elissa Gershowitz, Stacey Nichols Kim, Theresa Trinder, Laura Woollett
Editorial Assistant: Becky Ticotsky
Senior Editorial Manager: Sheila Neylon

Printed in U.S.A.

ISBN 0-8388-2824-8
978-0-8388-2824-X
1 2 3 4 5 CURW 11 10 09 08 07

Contents

Lesson 1

Word List

Study the definitions of the words below; then do the exercises for the lesson.

affection
ə fek´ shən

n. A fond or tender feeling.
Hugging is one way to show **affection**.
affectionate *adj.* Gentle and loving.
My cousin took my hand and gave it an **affectionate** squeeze.

appeal
ə pēl´

v. 1. To make an earnest request; to ask.
Three students **appealed** for more time to finish the work.
2. To be of interest to; to be attractive to.
This very funny movie will **appeal** to children of all ages.
n. 1. An earnest request for help.
The letter contained an **appeal** for money to provide shelters for the homeless.
2. The power to attract or be of interest.
Neither the liver and onions nor the meatloaf had much **appeal**.

clasp
klasp

v. To grasp or hold tightly.
The dancers **clasped** hands and circled the maypole.
n. 1. A strong grasp or hold.
The nurse gently removed the doll from the toddler's **clasp**.
2. Something, as a hook or fastener, that holds two parts together.
The necklace has a **clasp** in the shape of a snake biting its tail.

conspicuous
kən spik´ yo͞o əs

adj. Easily or plainly seen.
His great height made him **conspicuous** in any crowd.

contribute
kən trib´ yo͞ot

v. 1. To give along with others who are giving.
I **contributed** a spinach salad to the potluck supper.
2. To have a part in bringing about.
Exercise **contributes** greatly to good health
contribution *n.* (kän tri byo͞o´ shən) That which is given.
The museum sent a thank-you note for the fifty-dollar **contribution**.
contributor *n.* (kən trib´ yə tər) One who gives.
Contributors to the new theater received free tickets for opening night.

declare
dē klâr´

v. To make known; to state openly.
"I will not seek reelection," she **declared**.
declaration *n.* (dek lə rā´ shən) A public statement.
The **declaration** read by the mayor stated that November was bicycle safety month.

eloquent
el´ ə kwənt

adj. Skilled at speaking or writing; having the power to move people.
Anne Frank's **eloquent** diary often moves readers to tears.
eloquence *n.* Skill at speaking or writing; the power to move people.
Dr. Martin Luther King's **eloquence** made him the obvious choice to lead the 1960s Civil Rights Movement.

exhibit
eg zib´ it

v. To show in public.
Local artists **exhibited** their paintings at the library.
n. An item or collection of items in a public show.
The most interesting **exhibit** in the museum was the dinosaur skeleton.
exhibition *n.* (ek sə bish´ ən) A large-scale public show.
Tickets for the **exhibition** of early automobiles go on sale next week.

ferry
fer´ ē

n. A boat that carries people and goods back and forth across a stretch of water.
The **ferry** will go out of service when the new bridge opens.
v. To move people or goods by boat across a stretch of water.
The boat owner who **ferried** us across the lake would not accept any payment.

immigrant
im´ ə grənt

n. A person who comes into a country to live there.
Many Polish **immigrants** settled in Chicago.

lofty
lôf´ tē

adj. 1. Very tall or high.
Lofty elm trees provided welcome shade on many American streets.
2. Noble in feeling or high in ideals.
Ending world hunger in our lifetime is a **lofty** goal.
3. Showing a too-proud or superior attitude.
The **lofty** way the diner spoke to the waiter made me feel uncomfortable.

pedestal
ped´ əs təl

n. A base or support on which something stands.
After communism collapsed in Russia, hardly a statue of Stalin was left standing on its **pedestal**.

persecute
pur´ sə kyo͞ot

v. To treat cruelly or harshly because of political, religious, or other differences.
The Kurds of northern Iraq were **persecuted** by the Iraqi rulers for wanting their own state.
persecution *n.* (pur sə kyo͞o´ shən) The state or condition of being persecuted.
Hitler's **persecution** of the Jews led to the murder of millions of innocent people.

poverty
päv´ ər tē

n. The state of being poor.
The food stamp program was started to help feed American families living in **poverty**.

unveil
un vāl´

v. 1. To remove a covering from.
The president of the American Red Cross **unveiled** the portrait of its founder, Clara Barton.
2. To make known or reveal for the first time.
The police chief will **unveil** a plan to reduce street crime at today's meeting.

1A Finding Meanings

Choose two phrases to form a sentence that correctly uses a word from Word List 1. Write each sentence on the line provided.

1. (a) let that person go free.
   (b) To clasp someone is to
   (c) treat that person badly.
   (d) To persecute someone is to

2. (a) If something is lofty,
   (b) If something has appeal,
   (c) it is hidden from view.
   (d) it has the power to attract.

3. (a) To exhibit something is to
   (b) To unveil something is to
   (c) understand it fully.
   (d) reveal it for the first time.

4. (a) Poverty is
   (b) Eloquence is
   (c) a condition of poor health.
   (d) the state of being poor.

5. (a) To speak in an affectionate manner
   (b) To speak in a lofty manner
   (c) is to show a too-proud attitude
   (d) is to show extreme shyness.

6. (a) a lever operated by the foot.
   (b) An exhibit is
   (c) a public showing.
   (d) A pedestal is

7. (a) entry into a country to live there.
   (b) Eloquence is
   (c) skill at speaking or writing.
   (d) Affection is

8. (a) understand it.
   (b) hold it tightly.
   (c) To clasp something is to
   (d) To contribute to something is to

9. (a) ask that person for help.
   (b) To ferry someone is to
   (c) To appeal to someone is to
   (d) give comfort to that person.

10. (a) A pedestal is
    (b) A contribution is
    (c) a person traveling on foot.
    (d) something that is given.

1B Just the Right Word

Improve each of the following sentences by crossing out the bold phrase and replacing it with a word (or a form of the word) from Word List 1.

1. My parents were **people who left their own country to come** to the United States.
2. The **boat that carries people across the river** leaves every hour on the hour.
3. The sundial, together with the **base on which it stands**, costs two hundred dollars.
4. There was a burst of applause when the artist **removed the covering from** her painting.
5. The president's **public statement** that the factory would not be closing was welcome news to the townspeople.
6. A heavy dessert would not **be of interest** to me after that big turkey dinner.
7. The generosity of the audience **was one of the things that led** to the success of the auction.
8. The **noble-sounding words** of Abraham Lincoln's "Gettysburg Address" made a deep impression on me.
9. Their unusual way of dressing makes them **stand out from those around them** in a crowd.
10. I have nothing but **fond and tender feelings** for you all.

affection
appeal
clasp
conspicuous
contribute
declare
eloquent
exhibit
ferry
immigrant
lofty
pedestal
persecute
poverty
unveil

1C Applying Meanings

Circle the letter of each correct answer to the questions below. Each question has from one to four correct answers.

1. Which of the following could be **unveiled**?
   (a) a statue
   (b) a cloud
   (c) a painting
   (d) a plan

2. Which of the following can be **declared**?
   (a) a winner
   (b) one's children
   (c) one's love
   (d) a holiday

3. Which of the following can be **contributed**?
   (a) money
   (b) time
   (c) clothing
   (d) space

4. Which of the following could be **ferried**?
   (a) hopes
   (b) fears
   (c) people
   (d) cars

5. For which of the following might someone be subjected to **persecution**?
   (a) driving too fast
   (b) having different beliefs
   (c) breaking into someone's home
   (d) belonging to a different race

6. Which of the following would be **conspicuous**?
   (a) a lighthouse on a cliff
   (b) a pebble on the beach
   (c) a billboard by the roadside
   (d) a purple house

7. Which of the following could be **exhibited**?
   (a) pottery
   (b) days
   (c) uncertainty
   (d) coins

8. Which of the following are always true of **immigrants**?
   (a) They speak more than one language.
   (b) They are poor.
   (c) They plan to live in a new country.
   (d) They leave their own country.

1D Word Study

Circle two of four words that are synonyms in each of the groups of words below. (Synonyms are words having the same or nearly the same meaning.)

1. tall	eloquent	hidden	lofty
2. understand	contribute	declare	state
3. show	return	exhibition	appeal
4. eloquent	moving	conspicuous	tired
5. contribute	request	return	appeal
6. fastener	base	poverty	pedestal
7. affectionate	fond	conspicuous	sad
8. persecution	anger	grasp	clasp
9. ferry	poverty	need	desire
10. clasp	immigrant	supply	fastener

1E Passage

Read the passage below; then complete the exercise that follows.

Lady Liberty

The Statue of Liberty is a symbol of freedom to people all over the world, and since 1886 it has welcomed **immigrants** who sail into New York harbor to begin a new life in the United States. Like many of them, Lady Liberty, as the statue is **affectionately** known, had to overcome some difficulties before reaching these shores.

The statue was a gift from the people of France to the people of the United States in honor of the friendship between the two countries and the one-hundredth anniversary of the American Revolution. But before the statue could be put in place, the people of the United States had to provide a **pedestal** for it at a cost of one hundred thousand dollars. That turned out to be no easy task. A fund-raising drive was launched and ran into immediate difficulties. Newspapers across the United States ridiculed the effort. They argued that since the French were sending over the statue, they should be the ones to pay the extra costs involved for the base.

Despite this opposition, the effort to raise the money continued. A forty-foot-high section of the right arm, with the hand **clasping** the torch of liberty, was sent to the United States and displayed at the 1876 Philadelphia **exhibition** marking the one-hundredth birthday of the United States. Visitors paid fifty cents to climb onto the balcony surrounding the torch. Many other fund-raising events were held, but even after several years, **contributions** fell far short of the total needed, and the future of the entire project seemed in doubt. Not until a newspaper **appeal** promised to print donors' names was the necessary money raised.

With the success of the project assured, the rest of the statue was finally shipped from France in pieces packed in over two hundred wooden crates, and the work of assembling it proceeded without further delay. A public holiday was **declared** on October 28, 1886, when the Statue of Liberty was at last **unveiled** before one of the largest gatherings ever assembled in New York City. The island where it stands is called Liberty Island and is reached by a short **ferry** ride from lower Manhattan. At just over 305 feet, the statue was the tallest structure in New York City. Though it is now dwarfed by the **lofty** skyscrapers of Manhattan, at the time it was the most **conspicuous** landmark in the city.

In the 1880s, people seeking a better life were flooding into the United States at the rate of one million a year. Many of them came from Russia and eastern Europe; they had been cruelly **persecuted** by their governments and were fleeing to safety. Others were escaping the **poverty** of their native lands in search of a more prosperous life in America.

The museum at the base of the statue contains a bronze tablet placed there in 1903. On it is a poem written twenty years earlier by Emma Lazarus, whose own family had fled Russia. The poem has captured the imagination of the American people and has become forever associated with the Statue of Liberty. It ends with these **eloquent** lines:

Give me your tired, your poor,
Your huddled masses yearning to breathe free,
The wretched refuse of your teeming shore;
Send these, the homeless, tempest-tost to me,
I lift my lamp beside the golden door!

affection
appeal
clasp
conspicuous
contribute
declare
eloquent
exhibit
ferry
immigrant
lofty
pedestal
persecute
poverty
unveil

Answer each of the following questions in the form of a sentence. If a question does not contain a vocabulary word from this lesson's word list, use one in your answer. Use each word only once. Questions and answers will then contain all fifteen words (or forms of the words).

1. What is the meaning of **lofty** as it is used in the passage?

2. What finally caused Americans to **contribute** the necessary funds?

3. What was done with the statue's arm in Philadelphia in 1876?

4. How can you tell that the author has a favorable opinion of Lazarus's poem?

5. What is the meaning of **appeal** as it is used in the passage?

6. Why were so many people able to attend the first showing of the statue?

7. What was the hope of people who came to America to escape the **poverty** of their homelands?

8. Why did the American people have to raise $100,000?

9. How is the torch of liberty supported by the statue?

10. How do visitors reach the Statue of Liberty?

11. What is the meaning of **unveil** as it is used in the passage?

12. Why do you think the United States has been called a nation of **immigrants**?

13. Why is the statue not such a **conspicuous** landmark as it once was?

14. Why would **persecuted** people want to come to the United States?

15. Do you think the people fleeing to the United States for safety in the 1880s felt **affection** for their governments? Why or why not?

FUN & FASCINATING FACTS

The Latin word for *foot* is *ped*, and several English words, such as *pedal* (a lever worked by the foot) and *pedestrian* (a person going on foot), come from it. Since a **pedestal** is a base that stands at the foot, or lowest part, of a statue, column, or similar object, you might think that *pedestal* comes directly from *ped*. Actually it comes from an Italian phrase, *pie di stallo,* which means "a foot (or lowest part) of a stall." Since the Italian word for *foot* comes from *ped*, it's true to say that the English word *pedestal* also comes from it, but in a roundabout manner.

An **immigrant** is a person who enters a country intending to live there. An *emigrant* is a person who leaves one country to settle in another. In the late nineteenth and early twentieth centuries, many people *emigrated* from Europe and arrived in the United States as *immigrants*.

Persecute and *prosecute* are similar sounding words that are sometimes confused even though they have quite separate meanings. To *persecute* someone is to make that person suffer because of political, religious, or other differences. To *prosecute* someone is to bring that person to trial for criminal acts.

Lesson 2

Word List

Study the definitions of the words below; then do the exercises for the lesson.

arrogant
ar´ ə gənt

adj. Showing too much pride in oneself.
You were **arrogant** to claim that you knew all the answers.
arrogance *n.* A feeling of too much pride in oneself.
Declaring that you are sure to win is another example of your **arrogance**.

boycott
bɔi´ kät

v. To join others in refusing to deal with a person or group.
Customers plan to **boycott** that store if it continues to overcharge.
n. The act of boycotting.
The fans called off their **boycott** when the teams agreed to lower ticket prices.

campaign
kam pān´

n. 1. A series of actions intended to accomplish a goal.
Picking up litter was the first step in the **campaign** to clean up the town center.
2. A series of military actions in a particular area.
General Sherman's four-month-long Atlanta **campaign** ended with the fall of that city on September 2, 1864.
v. To take part in actions planned to accomplish a particular goal.
Students who wish to **campaign** for class office must submit petitions.

ceremony
ser´ ə mō nē

n. A formal event held in honor of a special occasion.
The bride and groom exchanged rings during the wedding **ceremony**.

custody
kus´ tə dē

n. 1. Control over and responsibility for care.
Following a divorce, each parent may want **custody** of the children.
2. In the keeping of the police; in jail.
The new officer took the thief into **custody**.

degrade
dē grād´

v. To bring shame or disgrace upon.
By lying to cover up his cheating, Sam **degraded** himself even more.
degrading *adj.* Causing shame or disgrace.
Losing the trophy because one player had taken a bribe was a **degrading** experience.

detain
dē tān´

v. To stop or hold; to keep from going on.
The customs officers **detained** us while they searched our bags.

extend
ek stend´

v. 1. To reach out.
The conductor **extended** her arms as a signal to the orchestra to be ready.
2. To offer.
I wish to **extend** my apologies for behaving so badly.
3. To make longer.
The exhibition was so popular that the museum decided to **extend** it by a week.
4. To stretch or lie.
The property **extends** for a half mile beyond the river.

integrate
in´ tə grāt

v. To unite into a whole; especially to end the separation of races.
In 1948, President Truman **integrated** the armed forces of the United States.
integration *n.* (in tə grā´ shən) The act of uniting or bringing together, especially people of different races.
In the 1950s many people opposed the **integration** of restaurants and other public places.

segregate
seg´ rə gāt

v. To keep separate or apart.
Ranchers **segregate** sick animals from the herd to prevent diseases from spreading.
segregation *n.* (seg rə gā´ shən) The act of keeping separate or apart.
One of the goals of the Civil Rights Movement was to end racial **segregation** in the United States.

supreme
sə prēm´

adj. 1. The highest in rank or position.
Saddam Hussein was the **supreme** ruler of Iraq until his overthrow in 2003.
2. Of the greatest importance.
The mayor declared that eliminating homelessness was the **supreme** challenge for the city.

triumph
trī´ əmf

n. 1. A noteworthy success.
Helen Keller's graduation from college was a **triumph**.
2. The joy winning brings.
The dancer who was invited to audition shot a look of **triumph** at those who were not so lucky.
v. To win.
The winner of the national spelling bee **triumphed** over forty-nine other contestants.
triumphant *adj.* (trī um´ fənt) Joyful over a victory or success.
The **triumphant** skater was given a hero's welcome on her return from the Olympic Games.

vacate
vā´ kāt

v. To make empty, as by leaving.
We will **vacate** the house at the end of June to make way for the people moving in.

verdict
vur´ dikt

n. 1. The decision reached at the end of a trial.
The foreman looked grim as she announced the **verdict**.
2. A judgment or opinion.
The **verdict** on the new computer is that it does twice the work in half the time.

violate
vī´ ə lāt

v. 1. To break, as a law or a promise.
Working for another research company **violates** the agreement she made with her previous employer.
2. To treat in an improper or disrespectful way.
The vandals who **violated** the cemetery by knocking over gravestones had to restore it.
violation *n.* (vī ə lā´ shən) A breaking of or failing to keep something like a law or a promise.
Revealing the secret to your friends was a **violation** of the trust placed in you.

2A Finding Meanings

Choose two phrases to form a sentence that correctly uses a word from Word List 2. Write each sentence on the line provided.

1. (a) A look of arrogance is one that
   (b) A look of triumph is one that
   (c) shows the joy of victory.
   (d) shows acceptance of defeat.

2. (a) A violated rule is one that
   (b) A degrading rule is one that
   (c) cannot be broken.
   (d) causes shame or disgrace.

3. (a) A segregated test is one
   (b) that everyone must take.
   (c) that is greater than all others.
   (d) A supreme test is one

4. (a) Arrogance is
   (b) humor at one's own expense.
   (c) Custody is
   (d) a feeling of self-importance.

5. (a) An extension of an agreement is
   (b) A violation of an agreement is
   (c) the act of signing it.
   (d) the act of breaking it.

6. (a) the state of being held by the police.
   (b) Integration is
   (c) the state of being afraid without reason.
   (d) Custody is

7. (a) improve its quality.
   (b) To segregate something is to
   (c) To extend something is to
   (d) increase its length.

8. (a) a series of military actions.
   (b) A campaign is
   (c) A ceremony is
   (d) a prize given to the winner.

9. (a) To boycott a business is to
   (b) increase the number of its customers.
   (c) open it up to people of all races.
   (d) To integrate a business is to

2B Just the Right Word

Improve each of the following sentences by crossing out the bold phrase and replacing it with a word (or a form of the word) from Word List 2.

1. The speaker called on us to take part in the **organized refusal to attend performances** of theater companies that employ nonunion actors.

2. Greenpeace is **taking part in a series of actions** to stop the killing of whales.

3. The king of Norway presents the Nobel Peace Prize at a **formal event in honor of the occasion** held in Oslo.

4. The separate companies were **brought together and formed** into one large corporation.

5. The people in the courtroom eagerly awaited the **decision reached at the end of the trial**.

6. Conditions in the jail **take away the self-respect of** the prisoners housed there.

7. The immigrants were **kept from going on their way** by inspectors who demanded to see their papers.

8. Students felt that their privacy was being **treated in a disrespectful and improper way** when their lockers were searched.

9. **The separation of the different races** in public schools was outlawed in 1954.

10. During the fire drill, students **moved out of** the school in an orderly way.

11. The children will remain in the state's **care and control** until their parents can be located.

arrogant
boycott
campaign
ceremony
custody
degrade
detain
extend
integrate
segregate
supreme
triumph
vacate
verdict
violate

2C Applying Meanings

Circle the letter of each correct answer to the questions below. Each question has from one to four correct answers.

1. Which of the following are **ceremonies**?
   (a) the swearing in of a president
   (b) a wedding
   (c) the election of a president
   (d) a birthday

2. Which of the following can be **violated**?
   (a) one's health
   (b) a building code
   (c) one's privacy
   (d) an order

3. Which of the following would be a **triumph**?
   (a) landing people on Mars
   (b) winning a portable radio
   (c) receiving a standing ovation for a speech
   (d) ending world poverty

4. Which of the following can be **boycotted**?
   (a) tap water
   (b) a brand of soft drink
   (c) punishment
   (d) a grocery store

5. Which of the following is a **verdict**?
   (a) "Guilty."
   (b) "Be quiet!"
   (c) "Not guilty."
   (d) "I didn't do it."

6. Which of the following might a person **campaign** for?
   (a) someone running for Congress
   (b) lower taxes
   (c) a second helping of food
   (d) changes in a law

7. Which of the following can be **detained**?
   (a) a journey
   (b) a lawbreaker
   (c) a guest
   (d) a passenger

8. Which of the following can be **vacated**?
   (a) a hotel room
   (b) hope
   (c) a seat
   (d) a promise

2D Word Study

Antonyms are pairs of words whose meanings are opposite or nearly opposite. *Rise* and *fall* are antonyms. Both words have to do with movement, but in opposite directions. Circle two of four words that are antonyms in each group of four below.

1. timid	wealthy	supreme	arrogant
2. release	detain	campaign	decide
3. vacate	segregate	immigrate	integrate
4. supreme	weighty	degrading	lowest
5. verdict	exhibit	disaster	triumph
6. degrade	violate	obey	declare
7. occupy	vacate	boycott	return
8. point	extend	shorten	clasp
9. conceal	persecute	unveil	need
10. health	poverty	wealth	affection

2E Passage

Read the passage below; then complete the exercise that follows.

The Mother of the Civil Rights Movement

Many people believe that the Civil Rights Movement in America began on December 1, 1955, when an African American woman named Rosa Parks refused to **vacate** her seat on a Montgomery, Alabama, bus so that a white person could sit there. At that time local laws unjustly allowed African Americans to be treated as second-class citizens. Many hotels, restaurants, and even drinking fountains throughout the South were for whites only. And in Montgomery, the state capital of Alabama, as elsewhere throughout the South, city buses were **segregated**; the front ten seats were set aside for whites, and African American passengers had to ride in the back.

Because she found it **degrading** to have to sit in the "colored" section of the bus, Rosa Parks usually walked home from her job in a Montgomery department store. But on that winter evening, Parks was feeling tired and decided to take the bus home. Soon all ten seats in the front of the bus were occupied by white people, and when another white man got on, the driver told Parks and three others to give up their seats so that he could **extend** the "whites only" section. The three others gave up their seats, but Parks refused to move. The driver called the police, who took her into **custody**.

After being **detained** at the police station for three hours, Parks was released and ordered to appear in court four days later. There she was found guilty and fined ten dollars. Her lawyers appealed the **verdict**, and the case slowly began making its way through the courts.

Meanwhile, the battle for civil rights was also being fought in the streets of Montgomery. African American people **boycotted** the city's buses, resulting in heavy losses to the company. An African American minister from Atlanta, Georgia, Dr. Martin Luther King, Jr., found himself suddenly thrust into a position of leadership. Many white citizens felt that the boycotters were being **arrogant** in demanding equal treatment under the law, and there were numerous outbreaks of violence. However, Dr. King preached a message of nonviolence, urging his supporters never to use force even if they were attacked. The country was moved by his eloquence and could no longer ignore the racial injustice that had been previously taken for granted. The **campaign** lasted 381 days and ended on December 20, 1956, when the United States **Supreme** Court agreed with a lower court ruling that the Montgomery law **violated** the United States Constitution. In ordering the bus company to **integrate** its buses, the nation's highest court sent a powerful message that African American people could no longer be treated as second-class citizens.

It was clear that the movement sparked by Rosa Parks had **triumphed** when Congress passed the 1964 Civil Rights Act, which opened up public housing, schools, and employment to people of all races. In 1989, Parks was invited to attend **ceremonies** at the White House marking the twenty-fifth anniversary of its passage. In 2002, her former home in Montgomery was placed on the National Register of Historic Places. These were fitting honors for the woman who has been called the mother of the Civil Rights Movement.

arrogant
boycott
campaign
ceremony
custody
degrade
detain
extend
integrate
segregate
supreme
triumph
vacate
verdict
violate

Answer each of the following questions in the form of a sentence. If a question does not contain a vocabulary word from this lesson's word list, use one in your answer. Use each word only once. Questions and answers will then contain all fifteen words (or forms of the words).

1. How do you think African Americans were affected by the bus **boycott**?

2. What is the meaning of **extend** as it is used in the passage?

3. Why did Rosa Parks get home late on December 1, 1955?

4. What is the meaning of **custody** as it is used in the passage?

5. Why can one not appeal a **Supreme** Court decision?

6. How did **segregation** in the South affect African Americans?

7. What is the meaning of **campaign** as it is used in the passage?

8. How did local laws throughout the South **degrade** African Americans?

9. Why did some whites believe that the African American protesters in Montgomery were behaving **arrogantly**?

10. What was the **verdict** in Rosa Parks's first court case?

11. What was the result of the **integration** of Montgomery's buses?

12. What is the meaning of **triumph** as it is used in the passage?

13. What did those sitting next to Rosa Parks on December 1, 1955, do when they were told to move?

14. What are two things you might do if called upon to organize a **ceremony** honoring Rosa Parks?

15. What is the meaning of **violated** as it is used in the passage?

FUN & FASCINATING FACTS

Captain Charles Boycott ran the Irish estates of the Earl of Erne in the 1880s, a time of great poverty in Ireland. He refused to lower the rents of those living on the estates and threw those who couldn't afford to pay out of their homes. In an attempt to force him to change his harsh ways, the people of County Mayo banded together and refused to have any dealings with him. Servants would not work in his house, and shopkeepers would not supply him with goods. In a very short time the captain's name had entered the English language. To **boycott** someone or something is to join with others in refusing to have any dealings with that person or thing. The word soon spread to other languages and has the same meaning in French, German, Dutch, and Russian.

The word **campaign** entered the English language from Latin by way of French. It happened like this. The Latin word for "field" is *campus*. Soldiers on active duty are sometimes said to be "in the field"; thus, a series of military actions in a particular area came to be called a campaign. The meaning of the word has been expanded so that it no longer refers only to a military course of action. We now have voter registration campaigns, anti-drug campaigns, and campaigns to clean up our city streets and parks.

The Latin word *integer* means "complete" or "whole," and whole numbers such as 1, 2, 3, and 4 are known as *integers*. The word **integrate** is formed from this Latin word; to be *integrated* is to be made *whole* or *complete*.

The Latin word for a herd or flock is *grex* or *greg*. The word **segregate** is formed by combining this root with the Latin prefix *sed-* or *se-*, which means "apart from." To *segregate* a group is to keep it *apart from* the rest of the *flock*.

A **verdict** is a decision reached at the end of a trial. The person who announces the verdict must speak the truth, as the word itself suggests. It comes from the Latin *dicere*, "to speak," and the Latin *verus*, "true."

Lesson 3

Word List

Study the definitions of the words below; then do the exercises for the lesson.

abundant
ə bun´ dənt

adj. More than enough; plentiful.
If good weather continues, farmers can expect an **abundant** harvest.
abundance *n.* A great amount.
Natural gas supplies an **abundance** of power to the entire country.

arid
âr´ id

adj. Having little or no rainfall; very dry.
Much of North Africa is **arid** land.

distinct
di stiŋkt´

adj. 1. Not the same; different or separate.
Apples come in over two thousand **distinct** varieties.
2. Unmistakable; definite.
Chili peppers add a **distinct** flavor to this dish.

graze
grāz

v. 1. To feed on growing grass.
A small herd of cows **grazed** in the meadow.
2. To touch lightly in passing.
The snowball **grazed** my cheek but didn't hurt me.

hectic
hek´ tik

adj. Full of feverish activity, haste, or confusion.
After a **hectic** week of sightseeing, the tourists were glad to go home and relax.

horde
hôrd

n. A large group or crowd, especially one on the move.
Hordes of swimmers head for the pool in summer.

humid
hyo͞o´ mid

adj. Having a large amount of water or moisture in the air.
Residents escape the hot, **humid** weather by going inside where it is cool and dry.
humidity *n.* (hyo͞o mid´ ə tē) The amount of moisture in the air.
The **humidity** was so high that the slightest activity made us sweat.

incredible
in kred´ ə bəl

adj. Hard or impossible to believe.
It seems **incredible** that no one was injured in such a bad accident.

inhabit
in hab´ it

v. To live in or on.
Millions of bison once **inhabited** the great plains of America.
inhabitant *n.* (in hab´ i tənt) A person or animal that lives in a certain place.
Most of the **inhabitants** of California were born somewhere else.

peninsula
pə nin´ sə lə

n. A piece of land, connected to a larger land mass, that juts out and is almost completely surrounded by water.
Bays along the Baja **peninsula** provide shelter for several kinds of whales.

rural
roor´ əl

adj. Of or relating to the country and the people who live there.
The villagers believe that a shopping mall has no place in a **rural** area.

sanctuary
saŋk´ choo er ē

n. 1. A place of safety or shelter.
The temple was a **sanctuary** to those who were being persecuted.
2. Protection offered by such a place.
The shelter offers **sanctuary** to women fleeing violence in the home.

splendor
splen´ dər

n. Magnificence; brilliance of appearance.
The **splendor** of the palace at Versailles took our breath away.
splendid *adj.* Very impressive; magnificent.
The exhibition of American sculpture includes several **splendid** statues by Harriet Hosmer.

squalor
skwä´ lər

n. Filth; misery.
People lived in **squalor** after their homes were destroyed by the hurricane.
squalid *adj.* Dirty and unfit for living, especially as a result of neglect.
The newly arrived immigrants worked long hours in **squalid** conditions for very low wages.

terrain
tə rān´

n. 1. An area of land; a region.
After hiking for several days we knew the **terrain** quite well.
2. The surface features of a region.
The mountainous **terrain** of western Colorado attracts skiers from all parts of the country.

3A Finding Meanings

Choose two phrases to form a sentence that correctly uses a word from Word List 3. Write each sentence on the line provided.

abundant
arid
distinct
graze
hectic
horde
humid
incredible
inhabit
peninsula
rural
sanctuary
splendor
squalor
terrain

1. (a) Squalid areas are those (c) Rural areas are those
(b) with little rainfall. (d) away from large cities.

2. (a) a place where prisoners are held before trial. (c) A sanctuary is
(b) land almost completely surrounded by water. (d) A peninsula is

3. (a) Something that is abundant is (c) Something that is incredible is
(b) hard to understand. (d) hard to believe.

4. (a) dampness in the air. (c) Humidity is
(b) Terrain is (d) the condition of being hot.

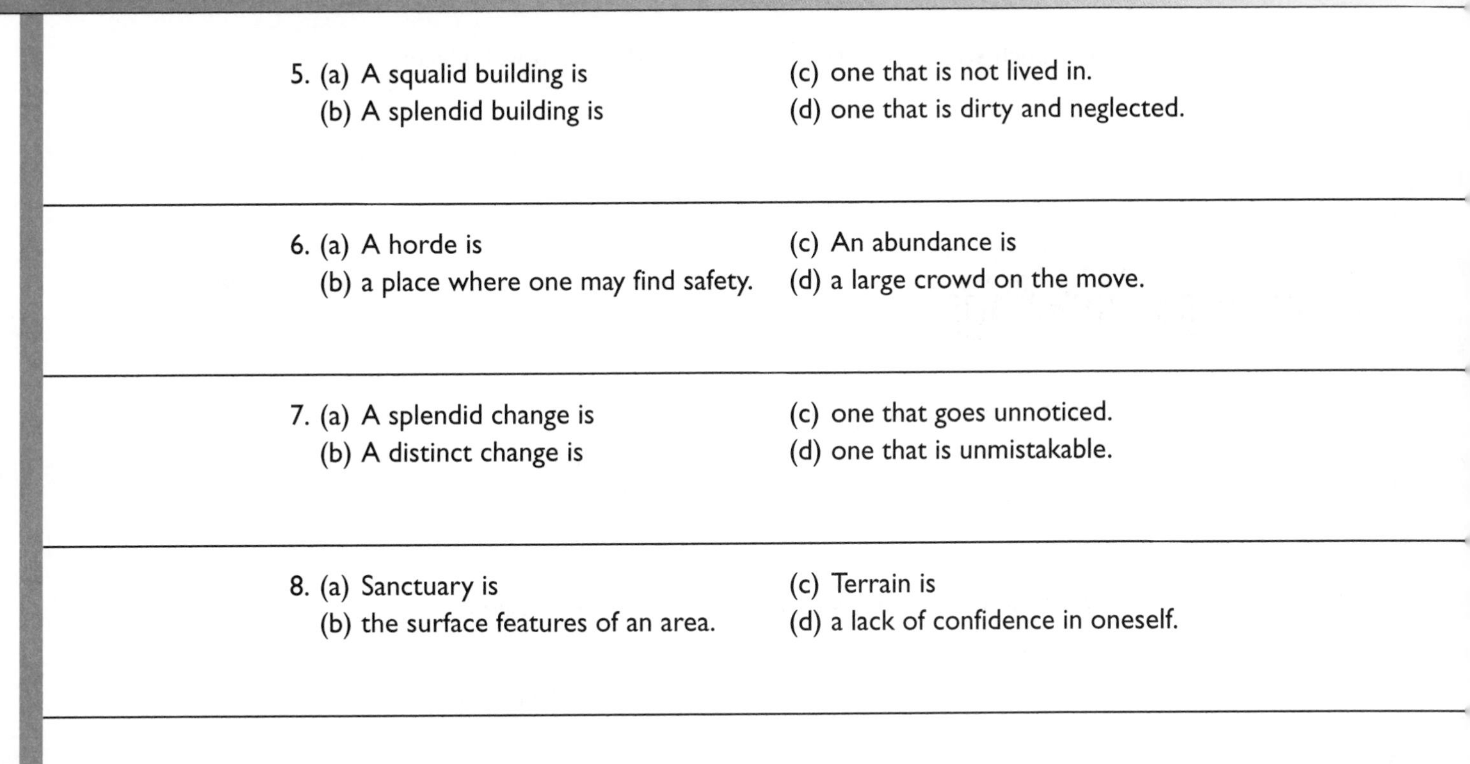

5. (a) A squalid building is
   (b) A splendid building is
   (c) one that is not lived in.
   (d) one that is dirty and neglected.

6. (a) A horde is
   (b) a place where one may find safety.
   (c) An abundance is
   (d) a large crowd on the move.

7. (a) A splendid change is
   (b) A distinct change is
   (c) one that goes unnoticed.
   (d) one that is unmistakable.

8. (a) Sanctuary is
   (b) the surface features of an area.
   (c) Terrain is
   (d) a lack of confidence in oneself.

3B Just the Right Word

Improve each of the following sentences by crossing out the bold phrase and replacing it with a word (or a form of the word) from Word List 3.

1. The Underground Railroad offered **a place of shelter** to slaves who were escaping to freedom.

2. The first ball from the pitcher **just barely hit** the batter's shoulder.

3. **Large numbers** of fans surrounded the stage door waiting for autographs.

4. Pitcairn Island has fewer than fifty **people who make their homes there**.

5. Her life was **full of feverish activity** because she worked at two full-time jobs.

6. Mark Twain wrote mostly about **life away from the cities and towns of** America.

7. The sounds of a flute and a trombone are quite **different from each other** so you can easily tell them apart.

8. Few crops can be grown where the land is **very dry and gets little rain**.

9. Monet's later paintings capture the **magnificent appearance** of his garden at Giverny.

10. Italy is a large **country that is almost completely surrounded by water**.

11. The rough **surface features of the land** made travel difficult.

12. Crops grow in **quantities that provide more than is needed** in such fertile soil.

3C Applying Meanings

Circle the letter of each correct answer to the questions below. Each question has from one to four correct answers.

1. Which of the following animals **graze**?
   (a) crocodiles (c) horses
   (b) sheep (d) cats

2. Which of the following would you find in an **arid** region?
   (a) ponds (c) snow
   (b) streams (d) cactus plants

3. Which of the following are **abundant**?
   (a) fish in the sea (c) food at a feast
   (b) water in the desert (d) trees in a forest

4. Which of the following might be found in **hordes**?
   (a) tourists (c) eagles
   (b) ants (d) trees

5. Which of the following might live in **splendor**?
   (a) a supreme ruler (c) a coal miner
   (b) a famous movie star (d) a person in custody

6. Which of the following places might be **hectic**?
   (a) a restaurant's kitchen (c) an airport over a holiday
   (b) backstage on opening night (d) a mall on a day in December

7. Which of the following might **inhabit** a tropical island?
   (a) Inuits (c) polar bears
   (b) penguins (d) monkeys

8. Which of the following could cause one to seek **sanctuary**?
   (a) fear (c) hunger
   (b) danger (d) thirst

abundant
arid
distinct
graze
hectic
horde
humid
incredible
inhabit
peninsula
rural
sanctuary
splendor
squalor
terrain

3D Word Study

Analogies test your understanding of the relationship between pairs of words. Example:

HOT : COLD ::

(a) hungry : tired
(b) light : heavy
(c) soaked : wet
(d) blue : yellow

When we read the analogy we say, "Hot is to cold as ______________ is to ______________."

The relationship between HOT and COLD is that they are opposites, or antonyms. So to find the answer, look for a pair of words that are also opposites. *Light* and *heavy* are opposites. None of the other pairs of words have this relationship. So the correct answer is (b).

Select the pair of words that most nearly expresses the relationship of the pair of words in capital letters. Circle the letter in front of the pair you choose.

HINT! Keep antonyms in mind as you do this exercise.

1. HUMID : ARID ::

(a) square : round
(b) sloppy : careless
(c) thirsty : hungry
(d) wet : dry

2. SPLENDID : SQUALID ::

(a) attractive : ugly
(b) loud : noisy
(c) lofty : towering
(d) lonely : alone

3. POVERTY : WEALTH ::

(a) love : marriage
(b) sickness : health
(c) age : beauty
(d) affection : friend

4. ARROGANT : HUMBLE ::

(a) cruel : kind
(b) hectic : eloquent
(c) abundant : plentiful
(d) friendly : loving

5. AFFECTIONATE : HATEFUL ::

(a) loud : noisy
(b) colorful : bright
(c) afraid : terrified
(d) abundant : scarce

6. VACATE : OCCUPY ::

(a) release : detain
(b) graze : touch
(c) appeal : demand
(d) exhibit : show

3E Passage

Read the passage below; then complete the exercise that follows.

Land of Contrasts

Thailand is a country about the size of France, with a population of over fifty million people. Nine-tenths of the people live in **rural** areas, away from Bangkok, the nation's capital and its only major city. Every year visitors from all over the world vacation in Bangkok, making tourism the country's number one industry, but most of them leave without seeing the rest of this fascinating country. This is a pity, for Thailand is a land of startling contrasts, made up of four **distinct** regions.

The northwestern region is the least accessible part of the country because of its mountainous **terrain** and many forests. Tigers, leopards, bears, and monkeys **inhabit** the more remote areas, while deer and buffalo **graze** on the grasslands that cover the lower slopes of the mountains. One of the world's great wildlife **sanctuaries** is located near Chiang Mai. This is the country's second largest city, although its population is only one-fiftieth that of Bangkok's. The two most important industries in this part of the country are lumber and tin mining.

The northeastern part of Thailand is vastly different from the northwestern part. It is by far the poorest region. Few crops grow there because of its **arid** climate and barren soil. Poor highways and a lack of railroads add to its problems. This region has little industry, and most of its people live in poverty. Many have left the land hoping to find work in Bangkok.

The most prosperous region is the great central plain where the soil is fertile and crops grow in **abundance**. Farmers there produce enough rice to feed the people of Thailand and still have some for export. Other crops include cotton, sugar, corn, tobacco, and peanuts. Bangkok is located on the southern edge of the central plain. It is a modern city with huge luxury hotels that have sprung up in recent years to accommodate the ever-increasing **hordes** of tourists. Many of them visit Bangkok to explore its rich cultural history. Among the city's many attractions are over four hundred Buddhist temples, five universities, and a huge Grand Palace where the rulers of Thailand once lived in royal **splendor**. But not all of the capital is **splendid**. Tourists seldom stray from the downtown area, with its many expensive shops and fine restaurants, into the more **squalid** parts of Bangkok where the city's poor live in overcrowded conditions.

The fourth distinctive region is the southern part of the country, which reaches to the Malaysian **peninsula**, within five hundred miles of the equator. This part of Thailand is mostly tropical rainforest with a **humid** climate and over two hundred inches of rain a year. It has an **incredible** variety of plant and animal life, including over five hundred different kinds of butterflies! It also has some of the finest beaches in the world to lure those tourists seeking a change from the **hectic** city life of Bangkok.

Visitors who spend a week or two in Bangkok may go home and tell their families and friends that they have seen Thailand. However, only those who have explored all four regions of the country can truly say, "I have seen Thailand."

abundant
arid
distinct
graze
hectic
horde
humid
incredible
inhabit
peninsula
rural
sanctuary
splendor
squalor
terrain

Answer each of the following questions in the form of a sentence. If a question does not contain a vocabulary word from this lesson's word list, use one in your answer. Use each word only once. Questions and answers will then contain all fifteen words (or forms of the words).

1. What is the meaning of **terrain** as it is used in the passage?

2. Why would most people in Thailand be unaccustomed to city life?

3. Which parts of Bangkok would *not* be shown in tourist brochures?

4. Why have so many large new hotels been built in Bangkok?

5. Why would you expect daily life in Bangkok to be more **hectic** than in Chiang Mai?

6. How can you tell that no one in Malaysia lives far from the sea?

7. What is one of the most **splendid** sights in Bangkok?

8. Why would Thailand's tropical rainforest be a good place to make a nature film?

9. What is the meaning of **distinct** as it is used in the passage?

10. Give an example of Thailand's **abundance** of animal life.

11. What is the meaning of **sanctuary** as it is used in the passage?

12. Which of the four regions of Thailand gets the least amount of rain? How do you know?

13. How many **inhabitants** does Bangkok have?

14. Why would you be likely to sweat a lot in the rain forest?

15. What is the meaning of **graze** as it is used in the passage?

FUN & FASCINATING FACTS

Horde comes from the Polish word *horda*, which in turn came from the Turkish word *ordu*, meaning "military camp" or "army." Centuries ago, the Turkish Mongols swept across Asia and eastern Europe in vast numbers, conquering the people in those areas. The word *horde* came to mean "a large number [of people] on the move." Don't confuse this word with *hoard*, which is a noun and means "a hidden supply or store." *Hoard* is also a verb that means "to save and store away in a greedy or secret manner." *Horde* and *hoard* are homophones; they sound the same but have different meanings and spellings.

The antonym of **rural** is *urban*. New York City is a large *urban* center; upper New York State, with its many farms and small towns, is mostly *rural*.

In Latin *sanctus* means "holy," and the original meaning of **sanctuary** is "a holy place." Churches, temples, and mosques were considered sanctuaries; people wanted by the law could find protection in such places because officers of the law would not enter them. The word *sanctuary* came to mean "protection offered by being in a holy place," and its meaning was later extended to include any place that offers safety. A bird sanctuary, for example, offers protection to the birds that nest there.

Lesson 4

Word List

Study the definitions of the words below; then do the exercises for the lesson.

aloft
ə lôft´

adv. Up in the air, especially in flight.
A strong breeze kept the kites **aloft**.

attain
ə tān´

v. 1. To reach; to arrive at.
Redwood trees **attain** heights of over 300 feet.
2. To achieve.
The library **attained** its lofty goal of raising ten thousand dollars for the repair fund.

buffet
bə fā´

n. 1. A piece of furniture with drawers and shelves for the display of plates, dishes, and bowls.
This splendid antique **buffet** contains a valuable collection of china.
2. A meal laid out for guests to help themselves.
The abundance of food at the **buffet** allowed people to go back for second or third helpings.
v. (buf´ ət) To pound repeatedly; to batter.
High winds and waves **buffeted** the ship during the storm.

elude
ē lo͞od´

v. To escape by being quick or clever.
The mouse **eluded** the cat by slipping through a crack in the wall.
elusive *adj.* (ē lo͞o´ siv) 1. Hard to find or capture.
The **elusive** outlaws were familiar with the terrain while those pursuing them were not.
2. Hard to explain or make clear.
Albert Einstein's connection between energy and the speed of light is too **elusive** for most nonscientists to grasp.

flammable
flam´ ə bəl

adj. Able to catch fire easily.
Children's night clothes must be fireproofed so they are not **flammable**.

hover
huv´ ər

v. To remain in place over an object or location.
Hummingbirds **hover** by beating their wings sixty times a second.

inflate
in flāt´

v. To fill with air or other gas.
Inflate the tires to the correct pressure.

jeopardy
jep´ ər dē

n. Danger.
Mountaineers who climb without partners put their lives in **jeopardy**.
jeopardize *v.* To put in danger of loss or injury.
Smokers **jeopardize** their health by smoking cigarettes.

moor
mo͝or

v. To hold in place with ropes or anchors.
After the sailors **moored** the boat to the dock, they went ashore.
mooring *n.* A place to which a boat or aircraft can be moored.
The hurricane tore many boats from their **moorings**.

plummet
plum´ ət

v. To fall suddenly toward the earth or to a lower level; to plunge.
The abundant harvest caused the price of corn to **plummet**.

pollute
pə lo͞ot´

v. To make impure or dirty.
Smoke from cars' engines **pollutes** the air of our cities.
pollution *n.* (pə lo͞o´ shən) The action of polluting; the state of being polluted.
The careless dumping of poisonous chemicals caused widespread **pollution** of the soil.

propel
prə pel´

v. To push or drive forward.
Two engines **propelled** the speedboat.

stationary
stā´ shə ner ē

adj. 1. Not moving.
A **stationary** bicycle is used for exercise.
2. Not changing.
The price of admission to the ball park has remained **stationary** for the past couple of years.

superb
sə pʉrb´

adj. Of the highest quality; grand; splendid.
The view from the mountaintop was **superb**.

swivel
swiv´ əl

n. A fastening that allows any part joined to it to swing freely.
This chair has a **swivel** that enables it to turn in a full circle.
v. To turn freely around a fixed point.
Owls can **swivel** their heads to look behind them.

4A Finding Meanings

Choose two phrases to form a sentence that correctly uses a word from Word List 4. Write each sentence on the line provided.

aloft
attain
buffet
elude
flammable
hover
inflate
jeopardy
moor
plummet
pollute
propel
stationary
superb
swivel

1. (a) A buffet is
   (b) a sudden loss of control.
   (c) A mooring is
   (d) a piece of furniture for displaying plates.

2. (a) To attain something is to
   (b) To jeopardize something is to
   (c) stay away from it.
   (d) put it in harm's way.

3. (a) To swivel is to
   (b) fall suddenly to earth.
   (c) To plummet is to
   (d) avoid getting caught.

4. (a) A superb automobile is one
   (b) that is in need of repair.
   (c) that is not moving.
   (d) A stationary automobile is one

5. (a) A mooring is
   (b) A swivel is
   (c) a small hole that allows air to escape.
   (d) a fastening that allows parts to move freely.

6. (a) To attain something is to
   (b) let it go.
   (c) reach it.
   (d) To inflate something is to

7. (a) lose sight of it.
   (b) To elude something is to
   (c) To propel something is to
   (d) drive it forward.

8. (a) bring it onto dry land.
   (b) To moor a boat is to
   (c) To inflate a boat is to
   (d) hold it in place with ropes.

4B Just the Right Word

Improve each of the following sentences by crossing out the bold phrase and replacing it with a word (or a form of the word) from Word List 4.

1. I was pleased when I **finally achieved** my goal of doing twenty push-ups.

2. The telescope **swings in any direction** so that it can be pointed to any part of the sky.

3. You can **pump some air into** that air mattress with this bicycle pump.

4. It's easier to hit a target that is **fixed in one spot and doesn't move**.

5. Materials that are **quick to catch fire** should be segregated in a fireproof container.

6. One expects the food at four-star restaurants to be **of the highest quality**.

7. I attempted to **get away from** my pursuer by hiding in a doorway.

8. It was a great thrill when we went **up in the air** in a hot-air balloon.

9. I started to feel seasick as the waves **continued to pound over and over against** the boat.

10. The helicopter **stayed in the air while remaining in place** over the ship's deck while its cargo was lowered.

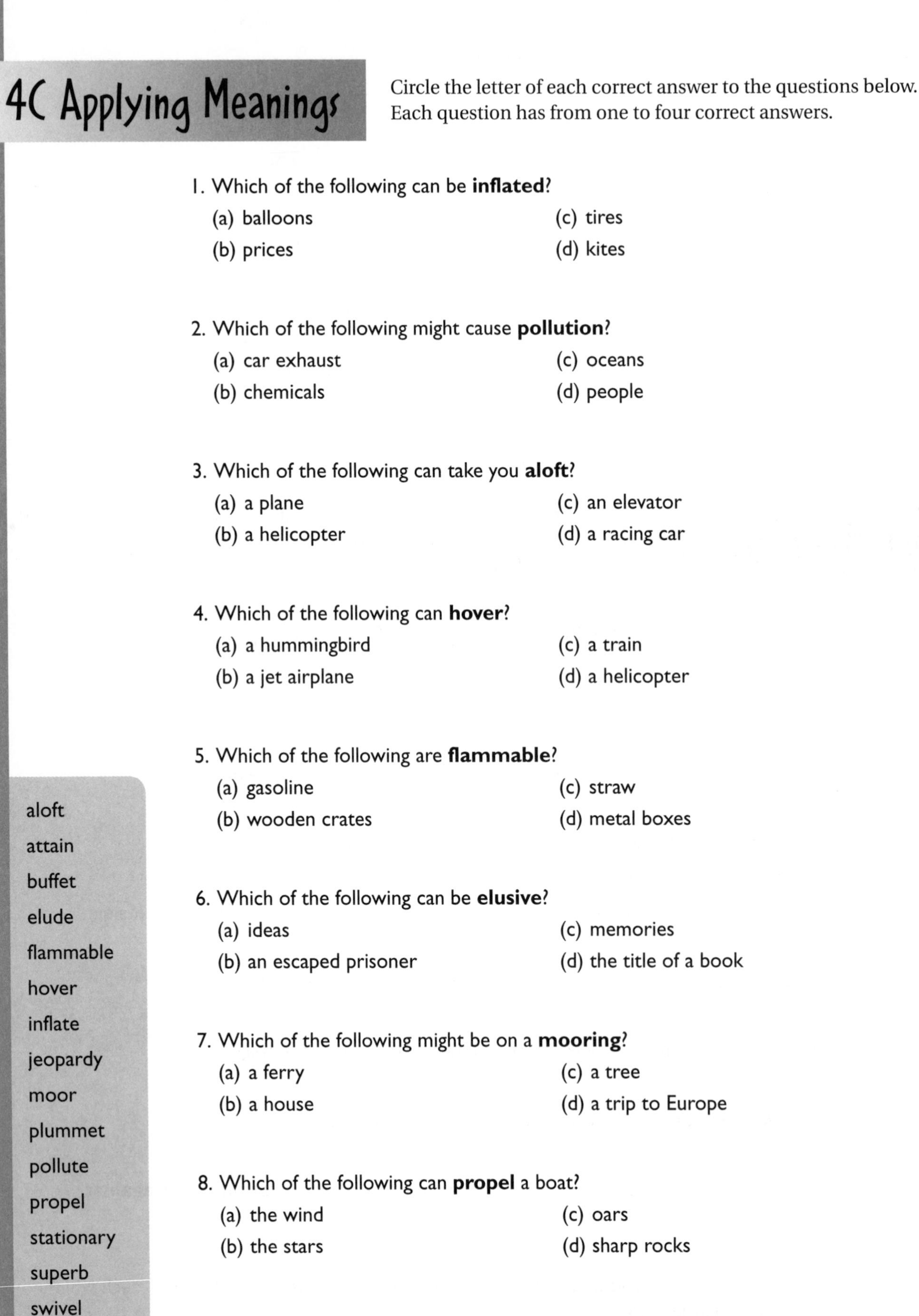

11. The water has been **made unfit for drinking** by the large amounts of chemicals dumped into it.

4C Applying Meanings

Circle the letter of each correct answer to the questions below. Each question has from one to four correct answers.

1. Which of the following can be **inflated**?
   (a) balloons (c) tires
   (b) prices (d) kites

2. Which of the following might cause **pollution**?
   (a) car exhaust (c) oceans
   (b) chemicals (d) people

3. Which of the following can take you **aloft**?
   (a) a plane (c) an elevator
   (b) a helicopter (d) a racing car

4. Which of the following can **hover**?
   (a) a hummingbird (c) a train
   (b) a jet airplane (d) a helicopter

5. Which of the following are **flammable**?
   (a) gasoline (c) straw
   (b) wooden crates (d) metal boxes

6. Which of the following can be **elusive**?
   (a) ideas (c) memories
   (b) an escaped prisoner (d) the title of a book

7. Which of the following might be on a **mooring**?
   (a) a ferry (c) a tree
   (b) a house (d) a trip to Europe

8. Which of the following can **propel** a boat?
   (a) the wind (c) oars
   (b) the stars (d) sharp rocks

aloft
attain
buffet
elude
flammable
hover
inflate
jeopardy
moor
plummet
pollute
propel
stationary
superb
swivel

4D Word Study

Some words are made up of more than one part. The part that comes before the base word is called a *prefix*. *Pre-* comes from Latin and means "before." Changing or adding a prefix can sometimes turn a word into its opposite.

Change each of the words below into its opposite by adding, dropping, or changing the prefix. Use one of these four prefixes, all of which mean "opposite of" or "not": *de-*, *dis-*, *un-*, *in-*.

1. conspicuous ____________________
2. inflate ____________________
3. upgrade ____________________
4. veil ____________________
5. inhabited ____________________
6. distinct ____________________
7. incredible ____________________
8. integrate ____________________
9. appealing ____________________
10. clasp ____________________

4E Passage

Read the passage below; then complete the exercise the follows.

A Different Way to Fly

Billboards standing along the highway are easily ignored, but a two-hundred-foot billboard floating across the sky grabs everyone's attention. That's why blimps are so attractive to advertisers with a product to sell or a message to communicate. But advertising is only one of the uses for a blimp.

Because they can be moved easily to different locations at varying altitudes, scientists use blimps for collecting samples used in the study of air **pollution**; the United States Navy employs them for offshore patrols; and one was even used to search for the **elusive** Loch Ness monster, supposed to inhabit a lake in Scotland.

A blimp is a large bag, called the envelope, that is **inflated** with helium gas. The blimp stays **aloft** because helium is seven times lighter than air. Once inside the envelope, the helium is left there unless the blimp needs major repairs. After the envelope has been filled, a cabin called a gondola is attached under it; this is where the crew and passengers ride. It is also where the light panels used for advertisements are attached. Computer graphics provide a dazzling display of pictures and words that can't be matched by any billboard.

Blimps are **propelled** by two engines, one on each side, and can **attain** a top speed of about forty miles an hour. Although slow in comparison to airplanes, blimps can do something most planes cannot: they can stop and **hover** in midair. This ability enables them to provide a **stationary** platform for the television cameras covering sporting events, giving viewers a bird's eye view of the action.

Blimps are not designed to take a **buffeting** from high winds, so they usually can go up only when the air is calm. When not flying, they have to be **moored** by the front end to a tall mast on a truck specially equipped for this purpose. Plenty of space is needed because the blimp has to be free to **swivel** clear of the ground when the wind changes.

In some cities it is possible to buy a ticket and go for a sightseeing trip in a blimp; because blimps fly so slowly and at such a low altitude, those on board enjoy **superb** views of the ground below. You might wonder what would happen if the envelope got a small hole in it. Would the helium rush out, causing the gondola to **plummet** to the ground? Passengers need not worry about that; their lives would not be in **jeopardy** if such a thing happened. Since the pressure of the air outside the envelope is greater than that of the helium inside, the helium doesn't easily escape. And since helium is not **flammable**, there is no danger of the envelope's contents catching fire. Flying in a blimp is safe and enjoyable.

Answer each of the following questions in the form of a sentence. If a question does not contain a vocabulary word from this lesson's word list, use one in your answer. Use each word only once. Questions and answers will then contain all fifteen words (or forms of the words).

1. Give two reasons why helium is used to fill a blimp's envelope.

2. For how long does the blimp's envelope remain **inflated**?

3. What is the meaning of **elusive** as it is used in the passage?

4. What would happen to the gondola if it became separated from the envelope while the blimp was in flight?

5. What is the meaning of **stationary** as it is used in the passage?

6. How can blimps be of use in scientific studies of the air?

7. What is the purpose of the **swivel** to which the blimp is attached?

8. Why does a blimp need to be **moored** when on the ground?

9. Why does a blimp's movement not depend on the direction of the wind?

10. What is the meaning of **attain** as it is used in the passage?

11. How could bad weather **jeopardize** a planned trip in a blimp?

12. Are engines essential to keep a blimp in the air? Why or why not?

13. Why do some advertisers think a blimp is a **superb** way to get their message across?

14. What is the meaning of **buffet** as it is used in the passage?

15. Why is a blimp useful as a platform for cameras for sporting events?

FUN & FASCINATING FACTS

The noun formed from the verb **inflate** is *inflation*. This word has a special meaning in economics. As wages and prices rise, a dollar no longer buys what it did earlier. A movie ticket once cost a quarter. What does it cost today? Twenty times as much? More? That's inflation!

Stationary is an adjective and means "not moving." *Stationery* is a noun and means "writing materials such as paper, envelopes, pens, and pencils." These two words are connected as the following story tells. Centuries ago in London, people sold goods from stalls set up near the London law courts. Some were permitted to stay in one spot for a short time only and then had to move to a new location. Others had special licenses that allowed them to stay in one place; they were called *stationers* because they did not move.

Many of these stationary stall holders sold writing materials to the people who worked in the law courts, and because they were called stationers, the writing materials they sold came to be called stationery.

By the early 1800s, spelling became fixed in its present form. The two different meanings were indicated by different spelling. *Stationary* was the adjective form and meant "not moving." *Stationery* was the noun form and meant "writing materials."

These two words are homophones; they have different meanings and spellings but are pronounced the same. It will keep you from confusing these two words if you remember the *a* is in the *adjective* form.

Review for Lessons 1–4

Crossword Puzzle Solve the crossword puzzle below by studying the clues and filling in the answer boxes. Clues followed by a number are definitions of words in Lessons 1 through 4. The number gives the word list in which the answer to the clue appears.

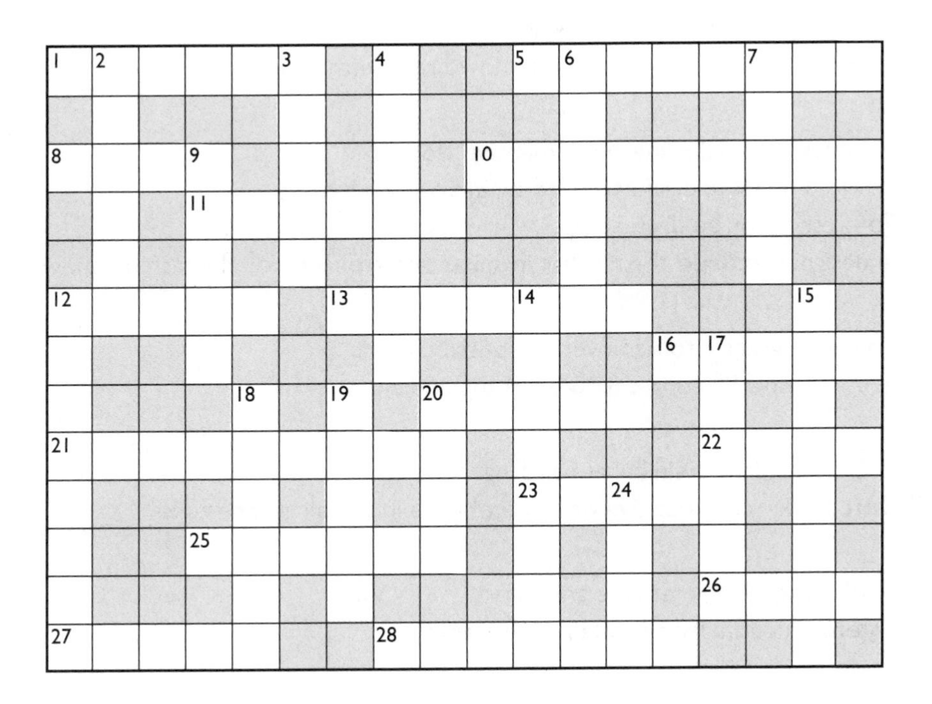

Clues Across

1. A request for help (1)
5. More than enough; plentiful (3)
8. To hold in place with ropes or anchors (4)
10. A fond or tender feeling (1)
11. To reach; to arrive at (4)
12. To grasp or hold tightly (1)
13. To break, as a law or promise (2)
16. Having a large amount of moisture in the air (3)
20. A large crowd (3)
21. To cause to suffer; to inflict hardship on (1)
22. People have a duty to ______ in an election.
23. To touch lightly in passing (3)
25. To make empty, as by leaving (2)
26. ______ and key
27. The 37th president of the United States
28. Responsibility for the care and control of (2)

Clues Down

2. To push or drive forward (4)
3. Very tall; high up (1)
4. To show in public (1)
6. To pound repeatedly; to batter (4)
7. Opposite of *dead*
9. Opposite of *to lower*
12. A series of actions to accomplish a goal (2)
14. Showing too much pride in oneself (2)
15. Unmistakable; definite (3)
17. To make known or show for the first time (1)
18. To stop or hold; to keep from proceeding (2)
19. Of or relating to the country (3)
20. Opposite of *there*
24. Having little or no rainfall; very dry (3)

Lesson 5

Word List

Study the definitions of the words below; then do the exercises for the lesson.

antic
an´ tik

n. (usually pl.) A playful or funny act.
The **antics** of the clown made the crowd roar with laughter.

attire
ə tīr´

n. Clothes, especially fine and expensive clothes.
One often needs special **attire** to be in a wedding party.
v. To dress up or be dressed up.
The designer **attired** the models in shirts and trousers for the fashion show.

captivate
kap´ ti vāt

v. To please greatly; to win over by special charm.
The cast's superb acting **captivated** the audience.

deft
deft

adj. Quick and sure; skillful at handling.
A **deft** juggler can keep five or more objects in the air at one time.

diligent
dil´ ə jənt

adj. Working with great care and effort.
Diligent students usually attain high marks.

eclipse
ē klips´

n. The total or partial hiding of one heavenly body by another.
An **eclipse** of the sun occurs when the moon passes directly in front of it.
v. To do or be better than; to outshine.
Her latest novel **eclipses** all of her previous work.

evolve
ē vôlv´

v. To develop and change gradually over time.
Some scientists think that modern birds may have **evolved** from dinosaurs.
evolution *n.* (ev ə lo͞o´ shən) The changes that take place as something evolves.
The **evolution** of aircraft from the Wright brothers' flimsy plane to the modern jet airplane occurred over an incredibly short time.

innate
in āt´

adj. Having from birth; occurring naturally rather than being learned.
Mozart's **innate** musical ability showed itself at a very early age.

inscribe
in skrīb´

v. To write, print, or etch into as a permanent record.
Most of the gravestones were simply **inscribed** with the person's name, date of birth, and date of death.
inscription *n.* (in skrip´ shən) The act of inscribing or what is inscribed.
Coins of the United States bear the **inscription** "E PLURIBUS UNUM."

posture
päs´ chər

n. The way one holds one's body; a pose or position.
You can improve your **posture** by throwing your shoulders back.
v. To assume a particular position, especially a pretended one.
They **postured** as my supporters while secretly campaigning against me.

shroud
shroud

n. 1. Something that covers or hides from view.
A **shroud** of mystery surrounds the couple's disappearance.
2. Cloth used to wrap a dead body before burial.
It used to be the custom to make a **shroud** from a long linen sheet dipped in melted wax.
v. To block from sight.
Dense fog on the river **shrouded** the tug boats.

stifle
stī´ fəl

v. 1. To cut off the air from; to smother.
Thick smoke **stifled** those who remained in the burning building.
2. To hold back; to check.
The spectators tried to **stifle** their yawns during the lengthy ceremony.

tentative
ten´ tə tiv

adj. Not fully worked out or final; hesitating or uncertain.
The deadline is **tentative** and may be extended.

tranquil
traŋ´ kwil

adj. Calm; peaceful.
The sea was **tranquil** with no hint of the approaching storm.
tranquility *n.* (traŋ kwil´ ət ē) The state of being tranquil.
Many authors prefer writing during the **tranquility** of early morning before anyone else is up.

versatile
vʉr´ sə təl

adj. Able to do many different things or to be used in many different ways.
She is a **versatile** musician who can play eight instruments.
versatility *n.* (vʉr sə til´ ə tē) The state or condition of being versatile.
The tomato's **versatility** and distinct flavor make it a favorite of many cooks.

5A Finding Meanings

Choose two phrases to form a sentence that correctly uses a word from Word List 5. Write each sentence on the line provided.

1. (a) To evolve is to
   (b) To posture is to
   (c) pretend to a position one doesn't really hold.
   (d) remain in one position without moving.

2. (a) make fun of that person.
   (b) To attire someone is to
   (c) dress that person.
   (d) To captivate someone is to

3. (a) A deft move is one that
   (b) is made in an uncertain way.
   (c) is repeated over and over.
   (d) A tentative move is one that

4. (a) gradual change over time.
   (b) Tranquility is
   (c) the ability to do many things well.
   (d) Evolution is

5. (a) A diligent person is one who
   (b) engages in foolish or playful acts.
   (c) A versatile person is one who
   (d) makes an effort to exercise great care.

6. (a) To stifle someone is to
   (b) To eclipse someone is to
   (c) fill that person with joy.
   (d) cut off that person's supply of air.

7. (a) Versatility is
   (b) Tranquility is
   (c) the state of being at peace.
   (d) an unwillingness to change one's mind.

8. (a) Something that is inscribed is
   (b) carried out in secret.
   (c) written into a permanent record.
   (d) Something that is innate is

9. (a) a covering for a dead body.
   (b) An eclipse is
   (c) a silly or playful act.
   (d) A shroud is

10. (a) To be deft
    (b) is to be greatly pleased and interested.
    (c) To be captivated
    (d) is to be held against one's will.

antic
attire
captivate
deft
diligent
eclipse
evolve
innate
inscribe
posture
shroud
stifle
tentative
tranquil
versatile

5B Just the Right Word

Improve each of the following sentences by crossing out the bold phrase and replacing it with a word (or a form of the word) from Word List 5.

1. The children's **playful acts** made their parents roar with laughter.

2. Your **ability to do so many things well** was what impressed the voters the most.

3. What is the correct **clothing that should be worn** for an awards banquet?

4. She **completely won over** the audience with her fine performance.

5. I admire the **very skillful** way you handled what could have been an embarrassing situation.

6. When is the next **time that the earth will pass directly between the sun's position and that** of the moon?

7. My aunt's exceptional vigor was **present from the time of her birth**; even as an infant she was active and strong.

8. Your backache is probably caused by your poor **way of holding your body**.

9. The bride **struggled to hold back** a giggle when the nervous bridegroom dropped the ring during the ceremony.

10. A thick fog **hid from sight everything that was in** the harbor.

5C Applying Meanings

Circle the letter of each correct answer to the questions below. Each question has from one to four correct answers.

1. Which of the following can be **versatile**?
   (a) a tool
   (b) a date in history
   (c) a performer
   (d) a thank-you note

2. Which of the following is an article of **attire**?
   (a) a vest
   (b) a walking stick
   (c) a hat
   (d) a pair of gloves

3. Which of the following might be an **antic**?
   (a) tickling someone
   (b) robbing someone
   (c) making funny faces
   (d) turning cartwheels

4. Which of the following could be **tentative**?
   (a) a movement
   (b) a suggestion
   (c) a proposal
   (d) a triumph

5. Which of the following have **evolved**?
   (a) plants
   (b) human beings
   (c) animals
   (d) automobiles

6. On which of the following might you find an **inscription**?
   (a) a pedestal
   (b) the front of a building
   (c) the inside cover of a book
   (d) an exhibit in a museum

7. Which of the following would you expect to be **tranquil**?
   (a) a hectic chase
   (b) a sanctuary
   (c) a rural scene
   (d) a rose garden

8. Which of the following is a **posture**?
   (a) sitting slumped over
   (b) dressing up
   (c) standing up with arms crossed
   (d) lying down

5D Word Study

Each group of four words below contains two words that are either synonyms or antonyms. Circle these two words; then circle the *S* if they are synonyms, the *A* if they are antonyms.

1. outshine	eclipse	vacate	posture	S	A
2. skillful	deft	humid	innate	S	A
3. tranquil	hidden	peaceful	versatile	S	A
4. exchange	purify	pollute	propel	S	A
5. swivel	charge	inflate	turn	S	A
6. hectic	distinct	rural	calm	S	A
7. squalid	diligent	versatile	magnificent	S	A
8. superb	splendid	distinct	enormous	S	A
9. danger	buffet	terrain	jeopardy	S	A
10. propel	detain	pollute	persecute	S	A

antic
attire
captivate
deft
diligent
eclipse
evolve
innate
inscribe
posture
shroud
stifle
tentative
tranquil
versatile

5E Passage

Read the passage below; then complete the exercise that follows.

A Born Artist

To exhibit one's work at the Smithsonian Institution in Washington, D.C., would be a high point in any artist's career; to receive such an honor at the age of fourteen is truly remarkable. Yet that was the age of the Chinese painter Wang Yani when her paintings were given their first American showing there in 1989. Hundreds of thousands of visitors came and were **captivated** by her pictures of animals, birds, and landscapes. And in the Smithsonian's Sackler Gallery, audiences were able to watch as Yani, barefoot and **attired** casually in shirt and denim shorts, walked on stage, and with **deft** strokes of the brush produced works of art right before their eyes. She did so with total concentration, seemingly unaware of the onlookers.

If fourteen seems a young age to receive so much attention, consider this: Yani's first exhibition, in her native China, was held when she was four! She has been working **diligently** at her art since the age of two; that was when Wang Shi Chiang first became aware of his daughter's interest in painting. Himself a well-known artist, he encouraged Yani by providing her with large sheets of paper, ink, and brushes, the traditional materials of Chinese painting. He never gave her a lesson and also discouraged her teachers at school from doing so. He believed such instruction would only **stifle** her imagination and prevent her from expressing her feelings freely. His faith in his daughter's **innate** talent was fully justified by her early success. In fact, Wang Yani's fame soon **eclipsed** her father's fame.

Yani's first subjects were monkeys. She became fascinated with their **antics** after a visit to the local zoo and painted hundreds of pictures of them. One of her favorites is thirty feet long and took her just four hours to complete. It shows 112 monkeys in various **postures**, each with a different expression.

As she grew older, she became more **versatile** and began painting other creatures such as birds, horses, and lions. Later, her style **evolved**, and she broadened her range of subjects to include trees, flowers, and, especially, landscapes. Her interest in landscapes is not surprising since Yani lives in a region of great natural beauty in southern China, with gently rolling hills, clear streams, and ancient temples. Not far away are the famous cone-shaped Guilin mountains, often **shrouded** in mist, and a favorite subject of the young painter. Yani paints what she feels about what she sees rather than simply what she sees, and in her paintings of the mountains she tries to capture the feeling of **tranquility** that she experienced while visiting the scene.

She often begins by spilling ink onto the paper, a method known as po-mo. She follows this with a few **tentative** strokes, then proceeds rapidly until the painting is completed, often in less than half an hour. Yani often includes an **inscription** in Chinese characters as part of a painting. A typical one reads, "Autumn is a withering season for the trees, but the animals are happy."

By the time she was sixteen, Yani had painted more than ten thousand pictures. You might wonder if she has time for other things. In addition to pursuing her studies, she reads for pleasure, especially Chinese literature. She also enjoys playing basketball and table tennis. Her other talents are singing and dancing, skills that she feels help her with her painting, for in a good painting, according to a Chinese saying, "the brush sings and the ink dances."

Answer each of the following questions in the form of a sentence. If a question does not contain a vocabulary word from this lesson's word list, use one in your answer. Use each word only once. Questions and answers will then contain all fifteen words (or forms of the words).

1. Why do you think Yani was able to produce more than ten thousand paintings by the time she was sixteen?

2. Why do you think Yani's first brush strokes are sometimes made in a **tentative** manner?

3. What feeling does Yani capture in her paintings of the Guilin mountains?

4. What subject **captivated** Yani when she was very young?

5. What ability is required in order to enjoy the **inscription** on a painting by Yani?

6. What is the meaning of **stifle** as it is used in the passage?

7. How can you explain Yani's ability to paint when she was so young and had never received any lessons?

8. What is the meaning of **posture** as it is used in the passage?

9. Has Yani always worn traditional Chinese **attire** when appearing in public?

10. How does Yani demonstrate her **versatility** in painting?

11. What is the meaning of **eclipse** as it is used in the passage?

12. Why would you expect a painting done by Yani when she was six years old to be different from one done when she was sixteen?

13. How does Yani's style of working enable her to finish a painting in such a short time?

14. What kind of monkeys' **antics** do you think Yani found amusing?

15. What is the meaning of **shroud** as it is used in the passage?

FUN & FASCINATING FACTS

The Latin word *natus* means "born" and forms the root of several English words. **Innate** qualities are those that seem to have been with a person since birth. *Prenatal* care is that given to a mother before the birth of her child. To be a *native* of a particular place means that one was born in that place.

Old English was the language spoken in England between 500 and 1200. A number of its words have survived, often with changed spellings and slightly altered meanings to become part of modern English. **Shroud** is such a word; it comes from *scrud*, an Old English word for a loose article of clothing that covered most of the body. The dead would usually be buried wearing the scrud they had worn in life, and in time the word, changed to *shroud*, came to mean "a covering for a dead body." As a verb it came to mean "to hide from sight" or "to cover."

Lesson 6

Word List

Study the definitions of the words below; then do the exercises for the lesson.

apparel
ə per´ əl

n. The things that are worn by a person; clothing.
Party goers dressed in their finest **apparel** for New Year's Eve.

appreciate
ə prē´ shē āt

v. 1. To see the worth or quality of.
I **appreciate** handmade lace edgings on pillowcases.
2. To increase in value.
The house we bought for $100,000 has **appreciated** to $180,000.

continuous
kən tin´ yo͞o əs

adj. Going on without stopping.
The **continuous** flow of traffic makes it impossible to cross the street here.

dissolve
di zälv´

v. 1. To make or become liquid.
Sugar **dissolves** easily in warm water.
2. To bring or to come to an end.
The members agreed to **dissolve** the chess club.

domesticate
dō mes´ ti kāt

v. To tame; to bring plants or animals under human control.
Some people claim that they can **domesticate** skunks, and that they make good pets.
domesticated *adj.* Brought under human control; tamed or cultivated.
The carrot is a **domesticated** form of a plant called Queen Anne's lace.

emerge
ē murj´

v. 1. To come into view; to appear.
A large brown bear **emerged** from the cave.
2. To become known.
The truth did not **emerge** until the trial was under way.

fiber
fī´ bər

n. 1. A thin, threadlike part of animal hair or plant tissue; also, an artificial thread that resembles this.
Cotton, wool, and rayon **fibers** can all be spun into yarn to make cloth.
2. An arrangement of body cells that forms muscles and nerves.
Red meat is made up of muscle **fiber**.
3. A food substance that provides bulk but is not digested.
Bran is a good source of **fiber** in one's diet.

function
fuŋk´ shən

v. To serve a purpose.
This couch also **functions** as a bed.
n. 1. The special purpose something is used for.
One **function** of a dictionary is to define words.
2. An important ceremony or gathering.
Following tonight's **function** to honor the retiring teachers, there will be a buffet.

hatch
hach

v. 1. To come or to bring forth from an egg.
A little yellow chick **hatched** last night.
2. To think up.
The children **hatched** a plot to scare their parents.
n. A small opening with a door or cover.
The **hatch** on the main deck flew open when the ship hit a reef.

inhibit
in hib´ it

v. To prevent from doing something or to prevent from happening.
Oil **inhibits** the formation of rust on metal.
inhibited *adj.* Held back because of shyness.
Inhibited people don't make friends easily.

minute
mī no͞ot´

adj. Very small; tiny.
A **minute** speck of dust in one's eye can be very annoying.

motion
mō´ shən

n. 1. Movement.
The **motion** of the train almost put me to sleep.
2. A suggestion on which members at a meeting must vote.
The **motion** to end further discussion was defeated by a show of hands.
v. To signal.
The shop owner **motioned** for the tourists to come in.
motionless *adj.* Not moving; stationary.
We eluded capture by remaining **motionless** when we heard the guards approaching.

sheathe
shēth

v. To cover with something that protects.
Metal workers will **sheathe** the ship's bottom with copper plates.

shed
shed

v. 1. To lose; to give up.
Cats **shed** hair in the summer.
2. To cause to flow.
The parents **shed** tears of joy when they heard their lost child had been found.
3. To throw off water without letting it soak through.
A raincoat should **shed** water.
4. To send out or give off.
The full moon **shed** a bright light.

transfer
trans fur´

v. To move, carry, send, or change from one person or place to another.
Transfer your notes to a fresh notebook.
n. (trans´ fər) 1. The act of transferring.
It is easy to **transfer** money from a savings to a checking account.
2. A ticket used for transferring from one bus or train to another.
A **transfer** from the subway allows riders to continue by bus without paying an additional charge.

6A Finding Meanings

Choose two phrases to form a sentence that correctly uses a word from Word List 6. Write each sentence on the line provided.

1. (a) it starts to flow.
   (b) If something appreciates
   (c) it increases in value.
   (d) If something hatches

2. (a) is one that is extremely tiny.
   (b) is one that eats only meat.
   (c) A domesticated creature
   (d) A minute creature

3. (a) A continuous movement is one that
   (b) goes on without stopping.
   (c) An inhibited movement is one that
   (d) is carried out quickly.

4. (a) come into view.
   (b) change from a liquid to a gas.
   (c) To dissolve is to
   (d) To emerge is to

5. (a) held back by shyness.
   (b) To be inhibited is to be
   (c) To be in motion is to be
   (d) occupied by living creatures.

6. (a) To transfer something is to
   (b) add to it.
   (c) move it to a different place.
   (d) To shed something is to

7. (a) Fiber is
   (b) a food substance that provides bulk.
   (c) Apparel is
   (d) the purpose for which something is used.

8. (a) A hatch is
   (b) a building used for storage.
   (c) a small covered opening.
   (d) A function is

apparel
appreciate
continuous
dissolve
domesticate
emerge
fiber
function
hatch
inhibit
minute
motion
sheathe
shed
transfer

6B Just the Right Word

Improve each of the following sentences by crossing out the bold phrase and replacing it with a word (or a form of the word) from Word List 6.

1. Cold weather **slows down** a plant's growth.

2. A duck's oiled feathers **stay dry inside by keeping out** water.

3. A lively discussion followed the **suggestion, on which those at the meeting had to vote**, that the club launch a campaign to attract new members.

4. The store sells only women's **articles of clothing**.

5. The dog was probably the first animal to be **tamed and brought under human control**.

6. It snowed **without a break** all weekend.

7. The baby turtles are starting to **break out of their shells**.

8. She **became known** as one of the most eloquent speakers in the Senate.

9. Electric wire is **protected by being covered** in plastic.

10. Eleanor's **move from her old school** to Lincoln High ensured that she could take the computer courses she wanted.

11. I **see the value of** what you are trying to do for us.

12. A single **thin thread made of wool** found at the crime scene matched those taken from the sweater of the suspect.

13. Two orange crates placed side by side **were put to use** as a table.

6C Applying Meanings

Circle the letter of each correct answer to the questions below. Each question has from one to four correct answers.

1. Which of the following are items of **apparel**?
   (a) hats
   (b) suitcases
   (c) suits
   (d) cars

2. Which of the following can be **dissolved**?
   (a) salt
   (b) a partnership
   (c) sugar
   (d) water

3. Which of the following is made from **fibers**?
   (a) rope
   (b) skin
   (c) a coconut
   (d) ice

4. Which of the following can be **hatched**?
   (a) an egg
   (b) a plot
   (c) a potato
   (d) an opening

5. Which of the following show that you **appreciate** something?
   (a) "That must have been hard to do."
   (b) "It's all your fault."
   (c) "I just love ballet!"
   (d) "Could you help me?"

6. Which of the following can be **shed**?
   (a) light
   (b) water
   (c) tears
   (d) blood

7. Which of the following are **functions** of television?
   (a) to entertain
   (b) to involve us in public events
   (c) to instruct
   (d) to sell products

8. Which of the following are **minute**?
   (a) a speck of dust
   (b) a grain of sand
   (c) a second
   (d) a one-celled animal

apparel
appreciate
continuous
dissolve
domesticate
emerge
fiber
function
hatch
inhibit
minute
motion
sheathe
shed
transfer

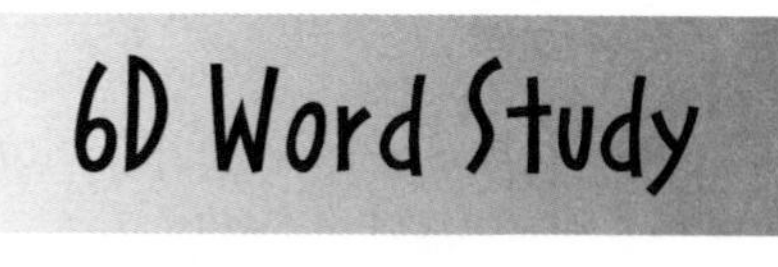

6D Word Study

In Lesson 4 you learned about prefixes. Another kind of word part is called a suffix. A suffix is added after a base word. One of the things suffixes do is change a word from one part of speech to another.

Change each of the nouns below into an adjective by adding the correct suffix and writing the word in the space provided. Both forms of all of the words in this exercise are from this or an earlier lesson.

1. affection ____________________
2. triumph ____________________
3. motion ____________________

Change each of the verbs below into a noun by adding the correct suffix and writing the word in the space provided.

4. inhabit ______________________

5. persecute ______________________

6. integrate ______________________

Change each of the adjectives below into a noun by adding the correct suffix and writing the word in the space provided.

7. eloquent ______________________

8. arrogant ______________________

9. humid ______________________

10. abundant ______________________

6E Passage

Read the passage below; then complete the exercise that follows.

The Story of Silk

"As soft as silk" we say, and with good reason, for silk is among the softest and finest of all fabrics. But where does silk come from? The silkworms that produce it come mainly from China, where they have been **domesticated** for thousands of years by silk farmers. According to legend, a Chinese empress known as the lady of Si-ling began the cultivation of silkworms in 2640 B.C.E., and the practice spread from China to other regions. Silk-producing areas today include Japan, Korea, India, Thailand, and Brazil.

The story of silk begins when the female moth lays its eggs, up to 500 of them at a time; they are **minute**, each smaller than the head of a pin. The eggs are stored in a cool place to **inhibit** their growth until the silk farmer is ready to use them. At that time they are **transferred** to a heated container called an incubator. Twenty days later, tiny silkworms start to **hatch**.

At this stage of its life, a silkworm does just one thing: it eats. And it eats just one thing—the leaves of the mulberry tree. A silkworm eats **continuously**, growing bigger and bigger until it seems ready to burst out of its skin. Then it stops eating and remains **motionless** for about a day, a sign that it will soon **shed** its old skin and replace it with a new one. This occurs four times altogether. When fully grown, at about six weeks, the silkworm has increased its size seventyfold. It now stops eating and prepares to enter the next stage of its life.

To accomplish this, the silkworm first **sheathes** itself in a cocoon, a kind of protective shell made from silk thread that it produces from a part of its body called the spinneret. During the three weeks it spends inside the cocoon, the silkworm turns into a fully grown moth. It has no teeth, so it cannot eat its way out; instead, it produces a liquid that **dissolves** the silk, making a hole in the cocoon. Then it slowly pulls itself through the hole. Once it has **emerged** from the cocoon, it is free to stretch its wings although they serve no useful **function**. Centuries of careful breeding have resulted in the silk moth's wings being so feeble that it cannot fly.

Most silkworms, however, do not survive to become moths. The few that do are used for breeding. The rest of the cocoons are taken by the farmer and heated in an oven to kill the silkworm inside; the silk, which is up to a mile long, is carefully unwound from the cocoon by machines. It can then be spun and woven into cloth to make men's and women's **apparel**, as well as upholstery, sheets, curtain materials, and even carpets.

Silk is the strongest of all natural **fibers**. It is also light in weight, warmer than cotton, rayon, or linen, and wrinkle resistant. These qualities, together with its incredible softness, make it highly desirable to those who **appreciate** the finer things in life.

Answer each of the following questions in the form of a sentence. If a question does not contain a vocabulary word from this lesson's word list, use one in your answer. Use each word only once. Questions and answers will then contain all fifteen words (or forms of the words).

1. What is the meaning of **hatch** as it is used in the passage?

2. What are blouses, dresses, scarves, and shirts?

3. What is the meaning of **emerge** as it is used in the passage?

4. Why is a cocoon that produces a live silk moth useless to the silk farmer?

5. What is the meaning of **function** as it is used in the passage?

6. Why does the incubator used by the silk farmer not need to be large?

7. Why do you think the silkworm's size increases so rapidly?

8. What is the meaning of **shed** as it is used in the passage?

9. What is the Chinese empress known as the lady of Si-ling known for?

10. How does the silkworm protect itself while it changes into a moth?

11. What does the silk farmer do with cocoons not needed for breeding purposes?

12. What effect does a cool temperature have on the growth of the silk moth's eggs?

13. How can one tell that a silkworm has outgrown its old skin and will shed it?

14. What is the meaning of **appreciate** as it is used in the passage?

15. What do silk, rayon, and wool have in common?

FUN & FASCINATING FACTS

Continuous means "going on without stopping." *Continual* means "happening over and over again." When a telephone rings *continuously*, it does so without stopping, perhaps because no one answers and the person calling does not hang up. When a telephone rings *continually*, it starts to ring again as soon as one call ends, and this goes on repeatedly for some time.

The adjective **minute** is pronounced mī no͞ot´. A *minute* amount is one that is very small. The noun *minute* is pronounced min´ it. (There are sixty *minutes* in an hour.)

To **sheathe** something is to cover it for protection. A *sheath* is a case that fits over something, such as the blade of a knife. Note that *sheathe* rhymes with *breathe* and *sheath* rhymes with *teeth.*

Lesson 7

Word List

Study the definitions of the words below; then do the exercises for the lesson.

brawl
brôl

n. A rough, noisy fight.
A **brawl** broke out when one of the workers accused another of stealing.
v. To fight noisily.
Players who **brawl** during the game are fined.

casual
kazh´ o͞o əl

adj. 1. Not planned.
Several friends got together for a **casual** meeting after the movie.
2. Not regular; occasional.
I have a **casual** job doing errands for my uncle when he needs me.
3. Suitable for everyday use; comfortable.
The store sells **casual** apparel for the beach.

constant
kän´ stənt

adj. 1. Not changing.
The function of cruise control is to keep the car at a **constant** speed.
2. Loyal; faithful.
The farmer's **constant** companion is an affectionate collie.
3. Without a pause; unending.
A small child requires **constant** attention.

excel
ek sel´

v. To do well; to be better or greater than others.
Babe Ruth **excelled** both as a pitcher and as a batter.

exhaust
eg zôst´

v. 1. To use up.
Lost on the mountain, the climbers **exhausted** their supplies after two days.
2. To tire out.
A ten-mile hike will **exhaust** most people.
n. The waste gases from an engine; *also*, the system that pumps out such waste gases.
The muffler is often the first part of the **exhaust** to wear out.

hardy
här´ dē

adj. Able to survive under bad conditions; tough.
Sage is a **hardy** plant that can be left outside during the winter.

mediocre
mē dē ō´ kər

adj. Of low to medium quality; barely passable.
Mediocre grades make it difficult to get into a good college.

monotonous
mə nät´ n əs

adj. Always the same; not varying; boring.
Making photocopies is **monotonous** work.
monotony *n.* Lack of variety resulting in boredom.
Switching tasks helps to relieve the **monotony** of assembly-line work.

originate
ə rij´ ə nāt

v. To bring or come into being.
The custom of sending Valentine cards **originated** in the 1800s.
origin *n.* (ôr´ ə jin) A beginning or coming into being.
What is the **origin** of the story that alligators live in the New York sewers?

punctuate
puŋk´ chōō āt

v. 1. To add marks such as commas and periods to writing to make the meaning clear.
Choose the best way to **punctuate** this sentence.
2. To interrupt from time to time.
Claps of thunder **punctuated** the evening.
punctuation *n.* (puŋk chōō ā´ shən) The use of marks such as commas and periods in writing.
Using a comma instead of a semicolon is a common error in **punctuation**.

ravenous
rav´ ə nəs

adj. 1. Very hungry.
The skaters were **ravenous** because they'd skipped lunch.
2. Eager for whatever satisfies one's needs or wants.
To be **ravenous** for praise shows a lack of confidence in oneself.

realistic
rē ə lis´ tik

adj. 1. Closely resembling real life.
This video game has very **realistic** race-car sounds.
2. Aware of things as they are; practical.
Running a Saturday car wash is a **realistic** way for the club to raise money.

soothe
sōōth

v. 1. To make calm and relaxed.
The principal tried to **soothe** the angry students by promising to consider their demands.
2. To relieve soreness; to make less painful.
Calamine lotion will **soothe** a sunburn.

stampede
stam pēd´

n. A sudden rush of animals or people, usually caused by fear.
A breeze carried the lion's scent to the antelope and began a **stampede** of the herd.
v. To take part in a stampede.
The crowd **stampeded** for the exit when someone yelled "Fire!"

veteran
vet´ ər ən

n. 1. A person who has served in the armed forces.
Veterans in their World War II uniforms marched in the Memorial Day parade.
2. A person with much experience.
The new director is a **veteran** who has been with the dance company from its beginning.
adj. Experienced.
We were fortunate to have several **veteran** musicians in our band.

7A Finding Meanings

Choose two phrases to form a sentence that correctly uses a word from Word List 7. Write each sentence on the line provided.

1. (a) a person who has much experience. (c) a sudden rush of frightened animals.
   (b) A veteran is (d) A brawl is

2. (a) A realistic offer is one that
   (b) is made in a joking manner.
   (c) A casual offer is one that
   (d) seems to make a lot of sense.

3. (a) A stampede is
   (b) a rope used by cowboys.
   (c) a rough and noisy fight.
   (d) A brawl is

4. (a) Monotony is
   (b) markings that make the meaning of writing clearer.
   (c) Punctuation is
   (d) a state of very great hunger.

5. (a) To stampede cattle is to
   (b) cause them to rush off in a panic.
   (c) To soothe cattle is to
   (d) put them out to feed on grass.

6. (a) A monotonous inspection
   (b) A casual inspection
   (c) is one that is thorough.
   (d) is one made without much thought.

7. (a) To exhaust someone is to
   (b) help that person relax.
   (c) forget about that person.
   (d) To soothe someone is to

8. (a) To excel at something is to
   (b) bring it to a sudden end.
   (c) To originate something is to
   (d) do it better than others.

brawl
casual
constant
excel
exhaust
hardy
mediocre
monotonous
originate
punctuate
ravenous
realistic
soothe
stampede
veteran

7B Just the Right Word

Improve each of the following sentences by crossing out the bold phrase and replacing it with a word (or a form of the word) from Word List 7.

1. He doesn't seem to be very **aware of how things really are** when he talks about his future plans.

2. The speech was **interrupted a number of times** by bursts of applause from the audience.

3. To spend winters in Alaska you need to be **tough enough to withstand difficult conditions**.

4. The rumor that the bank had failed caused a **panic in which everyone rushed** for the tellers' windows.

5. It takes a **person with years of experience as a** chef to run a smoothly functioning restaurant kitchen.

6. After being away for so long, the travelers were **very eager** for news from home.

7. By the time our supply of firewood was **used up**, warmer weather had arrived.

8. A hot bath will **ease the soreness of** your aching muscles.

9. Teenagers prefer clothes that are **suitable for everyday wear** and don't need ironing.

10. The telephone sales work is **boring because it lacks variety**, but it pays well.

11. Who **first came up with** the idea of growing plants in water?

12. Once set, the speed of the escalator was **fixed and did not change**.

7C Applying Meanings

Circle the letter of each correct answer to the questions below. Each question has from one to four correct answers.

1. Which of the following are **casual** clothes?
   (a) blue jeans
   (b) an evening gown
   (c) a dark blue suit
   (d) a track suit

2. Which of the following help musicians **excel**?
   (a) watching television
   (b) practicing every day
   (c) listening to their teachers
   (d) having innate ability

3. Which of the following is a **mediocre** grade?
   (a) A-
   (b) C-
   (c) B+
   (d) F

4. Which of the following would a **ravenous** person want to do?
   (a) eat
   (b) relax
   (c) sleep
   (d) exercise

5. Which of the following could **stampede**?
   (a) ants
   (b) a herd of cows
   (c) a horde of shoppers
   (d) a row of trees

6. Which of the following **punctuate** a piece of writing?
   (a) sentences
   (b) commas
   (c) adjectives
   (d) question marks

7. Which of the following could be **monotonous**?
   (a) a voice
   (b) a journey
   (c) a jaunt
   (d) a triumph

8. Which of the following might take part in a **brawl**?
   (a) newborns
   (b) hockey players
   (c) a herd of cattle
   (d) demonstrators at a rally

7D Word Study

Write a word from this or a previous lesson to complete each sentence. Use the explanation in parentheses to help you.

brawl
casual
constant
excel
exhaust
hardy
mediocre
monotonous
originate
punctuate
ravenous
realistic
soothe
stampede
veteran

1. To ________________ to something is to give along with others. (The word is formed from the prefix *con-*, which means "with," together with a root formed from the Latin word *tribuere*, which means "to grant or give.")

2. A(n) ________________ speaker is one who reaches out and moves an audience with the power of spoken language. (The word is formed from the Latin prefix e-, which means "out," together with a root formed from the Latin word *loqui*, which means "to speak.")

3. ________________ are people who leave their homeland and settle in another country. (The word is formed from the prefix *im-*, which means "in," together with a root formed from the Latin word *migrare*, which means "to depart.")

4. To ________________ different elements is to bring them together into a whole. (The word is formed from the Latin word *integrare*, which means "to make whole.")

5. A(n) ________________ story is one that is hard to believe. (The word is formed from the Latin prefix *in-*, which means "not," together with a root formed from the Latin word *credere*, which means "to believe.")

6. ______________________ qualities are those that a person is born with. (The word is formed from the Latin prefix *in-* (which means "in" as well as "not"), together with a root formed from the Latin word *natus*, which means "born.")

7. The ______________________ Court is the highest court in the land. (The word is formed from a root formed from the Latin word *supreme*, which means "highest.")

8. ______________________ conditions are those unfit for living because of dirt and other unhealthy conditions. (The word is formed from the Latin word *squalus*, which means "filthy.")

9. A(n) ______________________ is a decision reached at the end of a trial. (The word comes from roots formed from two Latin words, *verus*, which means "truth," and *dicere*, which means "to say.")

10. ______________________ animals live near or in people's homes. (The word is formed from the Latin *domus*, which means "home.")

7E Passage

Read the passage below; then complete the exercise that follows.

Home, Home on the Range

People may think they know all about the cowboys of the Wild West from watching westerns, but Hollywood movies do not give a very **realistic** picture of the life cowboys really led. Cowboy movies are **punctuated** throughout by gunfire, but real cowboys were mostly **mediocre** shots and seldom had reason to draw their guns; they carried them mostly for display. However, they did **excel** at riding and roping steers, essential skills for men whose job was handling cattle.

Although you would not know it from the movies, about a third of all cowboys were African American or Latino. In fact, the first cowboys came from Mexico and were called *vaqueros*, from the Spanish word *vaca*, which means "cow." The vaqueros contributed to the English language many of the words we associate with the Wild West, including *sombrero*, *mustang*, and *rodeo*.

Following the end of the Civil War in 1865, the vaqueros' numbers swelled with **veterans** who headed west to work on cattle ranches. Many were African Americans who found a greater degree of freedom in lands that were just opening up to settlement, and the rodeo offered them an opportunity to prove their worth. One of the earliest performers was an African American cowboy named Nat Love, who was born in a Tennessee slave cabin in 1854. As a boy of fifteen, he worked as a trail hand out of Dodge City, learning the riding and roping skills that made him a star of the rodeo. Perhaps the most famous rodeo performer was Bill Pickett, star of the Miller Brothers' Wild West Show, and the first African American admitted to the National Cowboy Hall of Fame.

Westerns usually show the cowboys in town having a good time, but the lives of the real cowboys were quite **monotonous** and were spent mostly working on the range. At that time, cowboys drove the cattle along trails that **originated** in Texas, where most of the cattle ranches were located, and ended in Kansas City, Abilene, or Dodge City. From there the cattle were shipped east on the recently built railroads.

Cowboys found **casual** employment as trail hands for these great cattle drives, which covered hundreds of miles and lasted up to three months. They were in the saddle from sunup to sundown as they herded the moving cattle. Cowboys kept a string of mustangs, the **hardy** wild ponies that roamed the plains, and changed to fresh mounts several times a day. Working hard in the open air made the cowboys **ravenous**, and when the evening sun went down, they were too **exhausted** to do anything but eat and sleep. Cowboys took turns during the night keeping a **constant** watch over the cattle, and whenever they seemed restless, the cowboys would **soothe** them by singing softly. Any loud noise or sudden movement could panic the herd and start a **stampede**. Then several thousand frantic cattle would suddenly charge off into the darkness with the hastily awakened cowboys in pursuit.

When the hands were paid at the end of the trail, they headed into town to spend their money. Those were the times when **brawls** might erupt. It was then that a cowboy's life was most likely to resemble what we see in the movies.

Answer each of the following questions in the form of a sentence. If a question does not contain a vocabulary word from this lesson's word list, use one in your answer. Use each word only once. Questions and answers will then contain all fifteen words (or forms of the words).

1. What is the meaning of **exhausted** as it is used in the passage?

2. Why did cowboys on the trail need to be especially alert during a thunderstorm?

3. How might western movies be made more **realistic**?

4. When do you think a cowboy might find himself locked up in the town jail?

5. Why were mustangs especially suitable for work on the cattle drives?

6. What is the meaning of **punctuate** as it is used in the passage?

7. Why do you think movies don't give an accurate picture of cowboys' lives?

brawl
casual
constant
excel
exhaust
hardy
mediocre
monotonous
originate
punctuate
ravenous
realistic
soothe
stampede
veteran

8. Why do you think sharpshooting was not featured at rodeos?

9. What is the meaning of **casual** as it is used in the passage?

10. What is the **origin** of *sombrero* and *mustang*?

11. Why do you think roping steers was a popular feature of the rodeo?

12. What is the meaning of **soothe** as it is used in the passage?

13. What do you think would be a welcome sight to **ravenous** cowboys?

14. How did the end of the Civil War affect the Wild West?

15. What is the meaning of **constant** as it is used in the passage?

FUN & FASCINATING FACTS

The noun form of the verb **exhaust** is *exhaustion*. (Several runners collapsed from *exhaustion* at the end of the race.) The adjective form is *exhausted*. (The *exhausted* rowers collapsed over their oars as they crossed the finish line.) A different adjective formed from this word is *exhaustive*, which means "thorough" or "complete." (After an *exhaustive* search, the missing book was found under the sofa.)

Medi means "middle" or "halfway" in Latin, and *ocris* means "mountain." These two words are combined to form the adjective **mediocre**, which means "halfway up the mountain." To be *mediocre* is to be neither very good nor very bad, neither at the top nor at the bottom.

Don't confuse **veteran** with *veterinarian*, a person qualified to give medical treatment to animals. Both words are sometimes shortened to *vet*.

Lesson 8

Word List

Study the definitions of the words below; then do the exercises for the lesson.

accompany
ə kum´ pə nē

v. 1. To go along with; to be together.
Thunder often **accompanies** lightning.
2. To play a musical instrument for or with.
The pianist offered to **accompany** the singer.

beneficial
ben ə fish´ əl

adj. Being of use; helpful; favorable.
A balanced diet is **beneficial** to one's health.

captive
kap´ tiv

n. One that is held prisoner.
The **captives** were closely guarded.
adj. Unable to escape or get away.
The hospital patients provided a **captive** audience for the mediocre comic.
captivity *n.* (kap tiv´ i tē) The state of being held against one's will; loss of freedom.
The giant panda rarely breeds in **captivity**.

convenient
kən vēn´ yənt

adj. Suitable for one's needs; making life easier or more comfortable.
The bus stop is **convenient** because it's close to my house.
convenience *n.* Anything that makes life easier or more comfortable.
The new tenants appreciated the central air-conditioning and other **conveniences** of the apartment.

ecstasy
ek´ stə sē

n. A strong feeling of emotion, especially joy.
Fans screamed in **ecstasy** when their idol appeared on stage.
ecstatic *adj.* (ek stat´ ik) Full of or causing ecstasy.
The winners were **ecstatic** when the judges read the names.

expanse
ek spans´

n. A wide, open area or surface; a stretch.
Wheat grows on the broad **expanse** of the Kansas prairie.

expedition
ek spə dish´ ən

n. 1. A long journey by a group to explore or do battle.
The **expedition** into the Brazilian rain forest lasted nearly a year.
2. A group that makes such a journey.
The **expedition** was attempting to find the origin of the Nile.

inept
in ept´

adj. 1. Clumsily or awkwardly expressed; not suitable for the occasion.
That **inept** remark you made at the funeral upset those who overheard it.
2. Lacking in skill or ability.
An **inept** handler damaged the contents of the crate.

interpret
in tur´ prət

v. 1. To translate into another language.
A native Parisian was hired to **interpret** the French minister's remarks for the audience.
2. To explain the meaning of.
Joseph offered to **interpret** the dream.
3. To understand in one's own way.
I **interpreted** your absence from the meeting as disapproval of what we were trying to do.

invaluable
in val´ yo͞o ə bəl

adj. Too valuable to measure; priceless.
The students' help in organizing the boycott was **invaluable**.

linger
liŋ´ gər

v. To be slow in leaving or going away.
The guests **lingered** in the hall, reluctant to go out into the cold.

retrieve
rē trēv´

v. 1. To get back; to recover.
Owners can **retrieve** their lost articles from the lost and found.
2. To find and bring back.
The puppy **retrieves** sticks the children throw in the pond.

skirmish
skur´ mish

n. A minor fight or battle.
Apart from a few **skirmishes**, both sides kept the cease-fire that had been agreed to.
v. To take part in such a fight.
The two sides began to **skirmish** before the major battle.

supplement
sup´ lə mənt

n. Something added to make up for something missing.
Those who eat a well-balanced diet do not need vitamin **supplements**.
v. (sup´ lə ment) To add to.
I **supplement** my allowance with earnings from a paper route.

territory
ter´ ə tôr ē

n. 1. A particular area of land.
A dog will defend its **territory**.
2. A land area under control of a particular group or government.
The island of Guam is a **territory** of the United States.

8A Finding Meanings

Choose two phrases to form a sentence that correctly uses a word from Word List 8. Write each sentence on the line provided.

1. (a) A supplement is
   (b) a part that is missing.
   (c) An expanse is
   (d) a part that is added afterward.

2. (a) whose worth is very great.
   (b) An invaluable object is one
   (c) that prevents one from going forward.
   (d) A convenient object is one

3. (a) To retrieve a package
   (b) is to go with it.
   (c) is to return it to the sender.
   (d) To accompany a package

4. (a) An expedition is
   (b) A territory is
   (c) a loss of one's freedom.
   (d) an area of land.

5. (a) To skirmish is to
   (b) To linger is to
   (c) add to what one already has.
   (d) take part in a minor battle.

6. (a) a lack of concern for others.
   (b) Captivity is
   (c) Ecstasy is
   (d) a feeling of great joy.

7. (a) one that is made clumsily.
   (b) A convenient move is
   (c) one that is made unwillingly.
   (d) An inept move is

8. (a) to deliver it by hand.
   (b) To retrieve a letter is
   (c) To interpret a letter is
   (d) to find it and bring it back.

8B Just the Right Word

Improve each of the following sentences by crossing out the bold phrase and replacing it with a word (or a form of the word) from Word List 8.

1. The students **added to** their box lunches with salads and milk from the cafeteria.

2. I will call on you tomorrow at ten if that is **a time that is suitable for you to see me**.

3. The organist will **play along with** the choir.

4. The crowd was **overcome with joy** when the home team scored in the final minutes.

5. Swimming can be **of great help** to those unable to do other forms of exercise.

6. The builder was so **lacking in the ability to do the work properly** that the job had to be done over.

7. Is it right to keep wild animals in **a state where their freedom has been taken away**?

8. A few shots were exchanged during the **minor battle**, but no one was injured.

9. The diners **were in no hurry to leave, so they spent some time** over their coffee.

10. Robert Peary's **long journey of exploration** reached the North Pole on April 6, 1909.

11. Your failure to answer the questions could be **understood by others** as an admission of your guilt.

12. To cross the great **wide open area** of the Pacific took many weeks by sailing ship.

8C Applying Meanings

Circle the letter of each correct answer to the questions below. Each question has from one to four correct answers.

1. Which of the following might **linger**?
   (a) a smell
   (b) a blow to the head
   (c) a headache
   (d) guests

2. Which of the following could be **invaluable**?
   (a) a work of art
   (b) a letter signed by Abraham Lincoln
   (c) a paper clip
   (d) knowledge of a foreign language

3. Which of the following might a **captive** do?
   (a) escape
   (b) elude capture
   (c) long for freedom
   (d) travel freely

4. Which of the following could be **interpreted**?
   (a) a long silence
   (b) a statement in a foreign language
   (c) a dream
   (d) a difficult passage in a poem

5. Which of the following are **territories**?
   (a) Lake Ontario
   (b) the island of Guam
   (c) the Hudson River
   (d) the Atlantic Ocean

accompany
beneficial
captive
convenient
ecstasy
expanse
expedition
inept
interpret
invaluable
linger
retrieve
skirmish
supplement
territory

6. Which of the following are **beneficial** to people?
   (a) injuries
   (b) fresh air
   (c) sleep
   (d) diseases

7. Which of the following are modern **conveniences**?
   (a) the automobile
   (b) indoor plumbing
   (c) the telephone
   (d) tables and chairs

8. Which of the following would be an **expedition**?
   (a) a journey up the Amazon
   (b) a visit to the store
   (c) a jaunt in a horse-drawn carriage
   (d) a voyage to Mars

8D Word Study

Select the pair of words that most nearly expresses the relationship of the pair of words in capital letters. Circle the letter in front of the pair you choose.

HINT! Keep synonyms in mind as you answer questions 1 through 5.

1. JEOPARDY : DANGER ::
   (a) abundance : scarcity
   (b) sanctuary : safety
   (c) mooring : boat
   (d) triumph : challenge

2. RETRIEVE : RECOVER ::
   (a) inhabit : inhibit
   (b) desire : hate
   (c) exhibit : show
   (d) weaken : strengthen

3. BLISSFUL : ECSTATIC ::
   (a) joyful : affectionate
   (b) starving : ravenous
   (c) skilled : inept
   (d) conspicuous : hidden

4. HELPFUL : BENEFICIAL ::
   (a) bold : inhibited
   (b) warm : humid
   (c) eloquent : abundant
   (d) harmful : dangerous

5. PRICELESS : INVALUABLE ::
   (a) fake : real
   (b) flammable : hot
   (c) glorious : triumphant
   (d) soothing : irritating

HINT! Keep antonyms in mind as you answer questions 6 through 10.

6. RURAL : URBAN ::
   (a) eloquent : elegant
   (b) arid : dry
   (c) tranquil : hectic
   (d) lofty : towering

7. ENCOURAGE : INHIBIT ::

(a) tire : exhaust
(b) soothe : irritate
(c) escape : emerge
(d) capture : captivate

8. DEFT : INEPT ::

(a) casual : occasional
(b) superb : versatile
(c) diligent : lazy
(d) melodious : musical

9. LIBERTY : CAPTIVITY ::

(a) restaurant : food
(b) wedding : ceremony
(c) peninsula : map
(d) variety : monotony

10. MINUTE : VAST ::

(a) lowly : supreme
(b) humid : hardy
(d) distinct : conspicuous
(d) shy : timid

8E Passage

Read the passage below; then complete the exercise that follows.

Sacagawea's Great Adventure

Imagine being snatched from your family and friends as a young teenager and taken far from home to be sold into slavery. That was the fate of Sacagawea, a Shoshone chief's daughter. The Shoshone people occupied what is now central Idaho on the western slopes of the Rocky Mountains. Sacagawea was taken **captive** in 1799, during a **skirmish** with a Hidatsa raiding party. She was then carried off to their village on the banks of the Missouri river, seven hundred miles to the east, in what is now North Dakota. It must have been a terrifying experience for the young girl, but because of her kidnapping and the events that followed it, she became part of American history. This is her story.

After she had been kidnapped, Sacagawea was sold to a French Canadian named Charbonneau, who lived in the Hidatsa village; she became his wife when she was about fifteen years old. In 1804 the Lewis and Clark **expedition** arrived at the village. Its purpose was to explore routes to the Pacific coast and report back to the United States government. Having set out from St. Louis six months earlier, its leaders decided that the Hidatsa village would be a **convenient** place to spend the winter. Since they knew they would be passing through Shoshone **territory**, they hired Charbonneau, who spoke the Shoshone language, to **interpret** for them. They decided that even though she had just had a baby, Sacagawea should also **accompany** them. Her presence with the baby would demonstrate to the Shoshone that the expedition's intentions were peaceful.

In April 1805 the party set out, traveling in canoes up the Missouri river. Sacagawea, her baby strapped to her back, proved to be an **invaluable** member of the team. She collected roots and berries to **supplement** the food stocks, and she was also able to add to the medical supplies for she knew which plants had a **beneficial** effect when someone fell ill. One day, Charbonneau's **inept** handling of the canoe overturned it, and some important records would have been lost had Sacagawea not **retrieved** them. Because of such acts, Sacagawea earned the respect of Lewis and Clark.

accompany
beneficial
captive
convenient
ecstasy
expanse
expedition
inept
interpret
invaluable
linger
retrieve
skirmish
supplement
territory

When they finally reached Shoshone country, Sacagawea had an **ecstatic** reunion with her brother, who was now a Shoshone chief. However, there was little time for her to **linger** among her own people as the expedition had to reach the Pacific before winter made travel impossible.

In mid-November the expedition reached the West Coast, and Sacagawea gazed for the first time at the vast **expanse** of the Pacific Ocean, of which she had heard stories since childhood. In March of 1806 the expedition began the return journey and reached the Hidatsa village in mid-August. Sacagawea remained there with her husband and child while the rest of the party continued east. Her great adventure was over. She had done things that must have been beyond her wildest dreams only two years before. She had been reunited with her brother, whom she had never expected to see again, and she had seen the Great Water. Although she had no way of knowing this, she had also earned for herself an honored place in America's history.

Answer each of the following questions in the form of a sentence. If a question does not contain a vocabulary word from this lesson's word list, use one in your answer. Use each word only once. Questions and answers will then contain all fifteen words (or forms of the words).

1. What were Lewis and Clark looking for six months after leaving St. Louis?

2. What is the meaning of **inept** as it is used in the passage?

3. How is it made clear that Sacagawea did not go willingly with the Hidatsa?

4. What is the meaning of **retrieve** as it is used in the passage?

5. What does the author indicate might have been the most striking feature of the Pacific Ocean for Sacagawea?

6. What is the meaning of **interpret** as it is used in the passage?

7. For how long was Sacagawea with the **expedition**?

8. Why was Sacagawea able to **supplement** the party's medical supplies?

9. What did the Shoshone do when they encountered the Hidatsa raiding party?

10. Why did Lewis and Clark believe that the presence of Sacagawea's baby might have a **beneficial** effect on the expedition?

11. What is the meaning of **territory** as it is used in the passage?

12. Why was Sacagawea **ecstatic** when she met the Shoshone chief?

13. How do you think Lewis and Clark felt about Sacagawea?

14. What is the meaning of **accompany** as it is used in the passage?

15. How do you know that Sacagawea was not eager to leave her brother?

FUN & FASCINATING FACTS

Translate and **interpret** have similar meanings; both mean to take words of one language and express them in another. *Translate* is the broader term and covers both written and spoken language. A speaker's words can be translated as they are being uttered; a book can be translated from one language into another. *Interpret* is a narrower term and is generally used only to refer to spoken words being expressed in another language.

A person who has had a frightening experience while in a plane might express relief at being back on *terra firma* after the plane has landed. The Latin for land is *terra*, and the phrase *terra firma* means "solid ground." The Latin *terra* occurs in several English words; among them are *terrain* (Word List 3) and **territory**, an area of land. The term *territory* is applied to those parts of the United States that have some form of self-government but have not been admitted to the Union as states. Guam and American Samoa are territories.

Review for Lessons 5–8

Crossword Puzzle Solve the crossword puzzle below by studying the clues and filling in the answer boxes. Clues followed by a number are definitions of words in Lessons 5 through 8. The number gives the word list in which the answer to the clue appears.

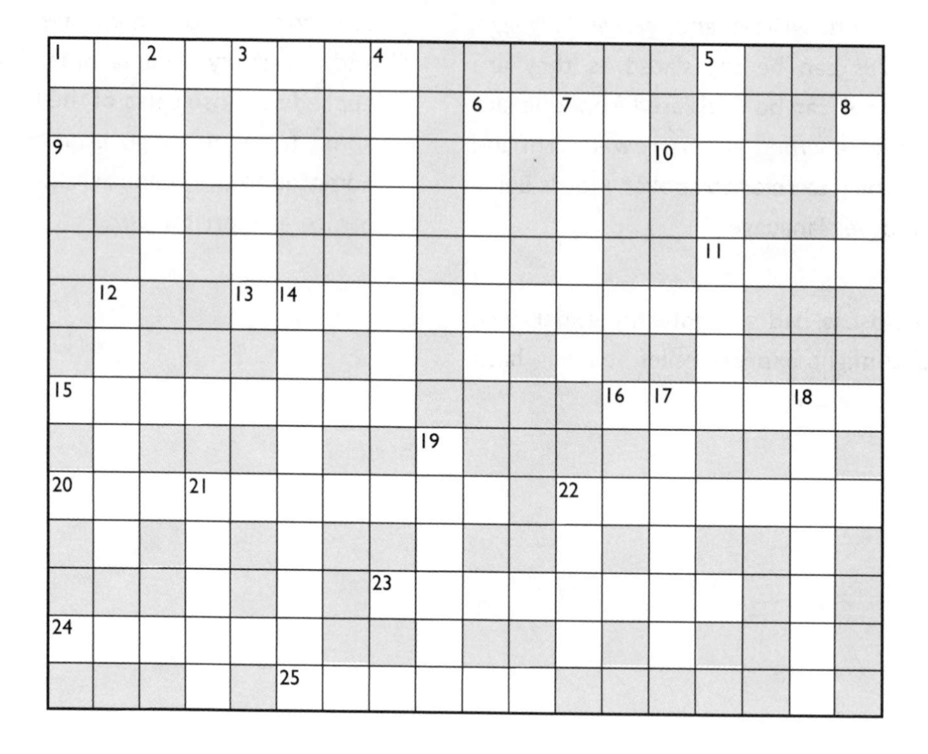

Clues Across

1. To move from one place to another (6)
6. One-twelfth of a foot
9. Clothes (5)
10. A small opening with a door or cover (6)
11. A small body of water
13. To bring under human control (6)
15. To write as a permanent record (5)
16. To come out of (6)
20. Of use; helpful (8)
22. A person with much experience (7)
23. To serve a purpose (6)
24. Not present
25. To change gradually over time (5)

Clues Down

2. A playful or funny act (5)
3. To cover or hide from sight (5)
4. To get back; to recover (8)
5. A sudden rush of frightened animals (7)
6. Present from birth (5)
7. A place where one could find sanctuary
8. To cause to flow (6)
12. To be in no hurry to leave (8)
14. To bring or come into being (7)
17. To make a movement of the hand or arm (6)
18. Worn so that one may see better
19. Suitable for everyday use; comfortable (7)
21. To do better than others (7)
22. What we do in elections

Lesson 9

Word List

Study the definitions of the words below; then do the exercises for the lesson.

accumulate
ə kyōōm´ yōō lāt

v. To increase in number or amount; to pile up, collect, or gather.
An inch of snow **accumulated** overnight.

aggravate
ag´ rə vāt

v. 1. To make worse.
The skater **aggravated** an old knee injury when she fell.
2. To anger or annoy.
That loud rock music from the club **aggravates** the neighbors.
aggravation *n.* (ag rə vā´ shən) 1. Annoyance; exasperation.
My **aggravation** increased as the noisy construction continued outside my window.
2. A source of annoyance or exasperation.
Deer and rabbits are a continuous **aggravation** to rural gardeners.

conserve
kən surv´

v. To save by using carefully.
Lower speed limits help **conserve** gasoline.
conservation *n.* (kän sər vā´ shən) The saving or protection of something through careful use.
A plan for the **conservation** of open space was unveiled at the town meeting.

contaminate
kən tam´ i nāt

v. To harm by contact with something undesirable.
Chemicals spilled last year continue to **contaminate** the lake.
contamination *n.* (kən tam i nā´ shən) The act of or result of contaminating.
Salt used on the roads in winter could lead to the **contamination** of ground water.

diminish
di min´ ish

v. To make or become smaller or less; to reduce.
Constant violations of the housing regulations will **diminish** the quality of life for all the inhabitants.

drastic
dras´ tik

adj. Severe; extreme.
Evil crimes receive **drastic** punishment in this new novel.

extravagant
ek strav´ ə gənt

adj. Spending, costing, or using more than is required.
Shawn's buying lunch for everyone was an **extravagant** thing to do.
extravagance *n.* 1. The quality of being wasteful or spending more than is necessary.
Emma's **extravagance** in early adulthood led to poverty later.
2. A thing that costs more than one can afford.
I admit the team jacket was an **extravagance**, but I couldn't resist buying it.

frugal
frōō´ gəl

adj. Careful in spending or using something.
The bill for the splendid wedding ceremony shocked my **frugal** relatives.

impurity
im pyōōr´ ə tē

n. Something that is harmful or dirty.
Filtering removes the **impurities** from water.

peril
per´ əl

n. Danger; something that is dangerous.
The sailor understood the **peril** involved in a solo crossing of the Atlantic Ocean.
imperil *v.* (im per´ əl) To place in danger.
A driver's ineptness **imperils** the passengers.
perilous *adj.* (per´ ə ləs) Dangerous.
An expedition into enemy territory could be **perilous**.

perpetual
pər pech´ o͞o əl

adj. Lasting or seeming to last forever or for a long time; continuous.
A **perpetual** calendar can be used year after year.

resource
rē´ sôrs

n. 1. A supply that can be used when there is a need.
Coal, aluminum, and lumber are natural **resources**.
2. Skill in dealing with difficult situations.
The committee's **resource** in working out the plan for integration is admirable.
resourceful *adj.* (rē sôrs´ fəl) Able to deal with difficult problems.
A **resourceful** person will triumph over difficulties.

substitute
sub´ stə to͞ot

v. To replace one thing or person for another.
Cooks sometimes **substitute** lemon for vinegar in salad dressing.
n. Something or someone that replaces another.
A flutist is a **substitute** for the violinist in tonight's concert.
adj. Acting in place of someone or something else.
The **substitute** teacher tolerated the class's antics.

sustain
sə stān´

v. 1. To keep up; to support.
Their firm belief that they would be rescued **sustained** them.
2. To suffer; to undergo.
The driver of the wrecked car **sustained** serious injuries.

vital
vīt´ l

adj. 1. Necessary for continued life or prosperity.
Oil is **vital** to the economy of the country.
2. Full of lively spirit.
Nelson Mandela's **vital** personality enabled him to survive years of imprisonment without bitterness.
3. Of the greatest importance.
It is **vital** that an official attend to the transfer immediately.

9A Finding Meanings

Choose two phrases to form a sentence that correctly uses a word from Word List 9. Write each sentence on the line provided.

1. (a) a source of annoyance.
   (b) An extravagance is
   (c) a source of danger.
   (d) An aggravation is

2. (a) that make a bad situation worse.
(b) that are extreme in nature.
(c) Drastic measures are those
(d) Frugal measures are those

3. (a) a gradual increase over time.
(b) Contamination is
(c) Conservation is
(d) contact with something harmful.

4. (a) a way of politely saying no.
(b) A substitute is
(c) something that is harmful or dirty.
(d) An impurity is

5. (a) to increase its amount.
(b) to spend it wastefully.
(c) To conserve wealth is
(d) To accumulate wealth is

6. (a) A substitute player is one who
(b) suffers an injury.
(c) A vital player is one who
(d) replaces another one.

7. (a) never seem to end.
(b) Diminished demands are those that
(c) seem reasonable.
(d) Perpetual demands are those that

8. (a) Something that is perilous is
(b) very dangerous.
(c) quite harmless.
(d) Someone who is resourceful is

9. (a) A resource is something
(b) that requires attention.
(c) An extravagance is something
(d) that costs more than one can easily afford.

9B Just the Right Word

Improve each of the following sentences by crossing out the bold phrase and replacing it with a word (or a form of the word) from Word List 9.

1. Many stores in the area **had to suffer through** a loss of business when the shipyard closed.

2. The taxpayers did not approve of the town's **wasteful spending of large amounts of money**.

3. The new medicine was recalled because it contained many **dirty and harmful substances.**

4. A thick layer of dust had **gathered little by little** on top of the piano.

5. A cook who is **careful not to waste anything** can make interesting dishes from leftovers.

6. The pain started to **become less severe** after a few days.

7. Our **abilities to deal with difficult situations** were tested to the maximum when our raft was propelled into dangerous rapids.

8. She seems so **full of lively spirit** that one forgets she is seriously ill.

9. The stage manager faced many **things that bothered or annoyed her** in trying to be ready for opening night.

10. By driving recklessly, you **placed in real danger** the lives of your passengers.

11. **Very severe** changes in the law are needed to deal with drunk drivers.

12. Unwashed hands can easily **bring dirt into contact with** food products.

13. The **careful use and saving** of water is extremely important on a long expedition.

accumulate
aggravate
conserve
contaminate
diminish
drastic
extravagant
frugal
impurity
peril
perpetual
resource
substitute
sustain
vital

9C Applying Meanings

Circle the letter of each correct answer to the questions below. Each question has from one to four correct answers.

1. Which of the following would **conserve** gasoline?
   (a) driving less often
   (b) traveling by bus or train
   (c) driving at slower speeds
   (d) buying smaller cars

2. Which of the following would **diminish** one's freedom?
   (a) being held captive
   (b) having one's driver's license taken away
   (c) joining the Navy
   (d) being released from prison

3. Which of the following are **vital** in a democracy?
   (a) voting in elections
   (b) advertising on television
   (c) learning about the issues
   (d) joining a political party

4. Which of the following might a **frugal** person do?
   (a) save used string
   (b) buy expensive presents
   (c) compare prices
   (d) travel by taxi

5. Which of the following are natural **resources**?
   (a) copper
   (b) iron
   (c) air
   (d) coal

6. Which of the following are **substitutes** for sugar?
   (a) honey
   (b) artificial sweeteners
   (c) chocolate
   (d) corn syrup

7. Which of the following are needed to **sustain** life?
   (a) oxygen
   (b) food
   (c) water
   (d) education

8. Which of the following might **aggravate** a sore throat?
   (a) eating ice cream
   (b) coughing
   (c) screaming
   (d) shouting

9D Word Study

Each group of four words below contains two words that are either synonyms or antonyms. Circle these two words; then circle the *S* if they are synonyms, the *A* if they are antonyms.

1. necessary	safe	drastic	vital	S	A
2. aggravate	linger	accumulate	annoy	S	A
3. impurity	expanse	peril	danger	S	A
4. substitute	replace	diminish	skirmish	S	A
5. extravagant	frugal	drastic	lengthy	S	A
6. resourceful	continuous	perpetual	anxious	S	A
7. increase	sustain	diminish	compete	S	A
8. waste	shed	conserve	contaminate	S	A
9. extreme	resourceful	realistic	drastic	S	A

9E Passage

Read the passage below; then complete the exercise that follows.

Water, Water, Everywhere

What sets our planet apart from all the others? Pictures from space show Earth to be the blue planet, its color coming from the water that covers about three quarters of its surface. To the best of our knowledge, ours is the only planet that can **sustain** life, and water is the reason. You'd think we would treat something so **vital** to our lives as a valuable gift, but sadly, that has not been the case. Except during times of drought, when we realize how precious it is, water is something we take very much for granted.

The water that makes up the earth's rivers, oceans, and lakes is always in motion. As it is warmed by the sun, water evaporates into the air and the vapor forms clouds, leaving behind the **impurities** that were dissolved in the water. As the vapor cools, it forms water droplets that eventually fall as rain. The rainfall **accumulates** in the earth's different bodies of water, where it is heated by the sun and evaporates once more. This process is known as the rain cycle, and it has gone on **perpetually** since it started—about 500,000 years after the earth was formed. It is nature's way of keeping the earth's supply of water clean. For billions of years it worked well, but with the growth of industry and the increase in population over the past two hundred years, the situation has changed **drastically**.

The standard of living that Americans enjoy exceeds anything our ancestors dreamed of. But the conveniences of daily life that we are accustomed to have been obtained at a terrible price. In our eagerness to make what we call progress, we have **contaminated** our rivers, oceans, and lakes by emptying the raw sewage from our toilets into them. We have **aggravated** the problem by allowing chemical pesticides and fertilizers used on crops to run off into our water supplies. We have also dumped poisonous chemicals into landfills so that in many places the water lying under the ground **imperils** the health of those who eventually drink it. As a result, the amount of clean water is **diminishing**.

Human beings have often demonstrated how **resourceful** they can be when there are problems to be solved. When we run out of something we need, we can usually find something else to take its place; however, there is no **substitute** for water. We have to learn to **conserve** this precious liquid as though our lives depend on it—because they do. An **extravagant** person is sometimes said to "spend money like water." Now, however, the time has come for us to learn to be **frugal** and spend our water as carefully as a penny pincher spends money.

Answer each of the following questions in the form of a sentence. If a question does not contain a vocabulary word from this lesson's word list, use one in your answer. Use each word only once. Questions and answers will then contain all fifteen words (or forms of the words).

1. What are three things that can **contaminate** water?

---

2. What is the meaning of **aggravate** as it is used in the passage?

---

3. What three ways can you think of to practice water **conservation**?

4. What is the meaning of **substitute** as it is used in the passage?

5. What happens to the quantity of clean water as water pollution increases?

6. What is the meaning of **vital** as it is used in the passage?

7. What remains after the **impurities** have been removed from water?

8. How would you describe the taking of twenty-minute showers during a drought?

9. Why is water our most precious natural **resource**?

10. What happens when poisonous chemicals **accumulate** in landfills?

11. How would you describe turning off the faucet when brushing one's teeth?

12. How can drinking from most rivers and ponds affect a person's health?

13. How would you describe an order that restricted families to only one gallon of water a day?

14. What is the meaning of **sustain** as it is used in the passage?

15. Has the rain cycle ever stopped since it began?

FUN & FASCINATING FACTS

To *preserve* something is to keep it from being harmed or used up. To **conserve** something is to use it carefully and without waste. To *preserve* the giant California sequoias means not cutting down a single tree; to *conserve* a forest means to cut down no more trees than can be replaced naturally.

When **substitute** is used as a verb, it is always followed by the preposition *for*. You substitute one thing *for* another. You never substitute something *with* something else. You do, however, *replace* something *with* something else.

Lesson 10

Word List

Study the definitions of the words below; then do the exercises for the lesson.

anticipate
an tis´ ə pāt

v. 1. To look forward to; to expect.
We **anticipated** having a good time at the party.
2. To be aware of and to provide for beforehand.
The speaker **anticipated** their questions by explaining the plan thoroughly.

bankrupt
baŋk´ rupt

adj. 1. Unable to pay one's debts and freed by law from doing so.
The store owner was **bankrupt** after the business failed.
2. Left without any worth or value.
The opposition party was **bankrupt** of ideas and received few votes.
v. To leave without worth or value.
His extravagances **bankrupted** him.

brief
brēf

adj. Short; not long-lasting.
The guests had time for just a **brief** visit, so they did not linger when it was time to leave.
v. To give a short explanation or set of instructions to.
An assistant **briefed** the mayor before the debate.
n. A statement, giving the main points in a case, for use in a court of law.
The attorney glanced at her **brief** before addressing the judge.

brisk
brisk

adj. 1. Quick; active.
The runners kept up a **brisk** pace at the start of the race.
2. Stimulating; refreshing.
The **brisk** wind blowing off the ocean felt good.

budget
buj´ ət

n. A plan for spending money during a certain period.
The extravagant dinner caused the tourists to overspend their weekly food **budget**.
v. To plan the use of carefully.
A part-time job may affect your schoolwork unless you **budget** your time.

compete
kəm pēt´

v. To try to win against others.
Five students **competed** for first prize.
competition *n.* (käm pə tish´ ən) 1. The act of trying to win against others.
Competition to get into a good college is keen.
2. A contest.
The team entered the **competition** even though it had little chance of winning.
competitor *n.* (käm pet´ i tər) One who competes against others.
Six **competitors** entered the race.

complicate
käm´ pli kāt

v. To make difficult.
An extra guest may **complicate** the seating for a formal dinner.
complicated *adj.* Not easy or simple; having many different parts.
The instructions are so **complicated** that no one could figure them out.

effect
ə fekt´

v. To make happen.
The new manager will **effect** many changes.
n. A result.
The aspirin I took for my headache had no **effect**.
effective *adj.* (ə fek´ tiv) 1. Bringing about the desired result.
Gargling with salt water is an **effective** treatment for a minor sore throat.
2. In operation; active.
A new dress code was **effective** the day school opened.
3. Making a strong and favorable impression.
People are likely to remember what an **effective** speaker says.

err
ʉr

v. To be wrong or to do wrong.
I **erred** when I accused you of lying.
error *n.* (er´ ər) A mistake.
Errors in punctuation are easily corrected.
erroneous *adj.* (ər rō´ nē əs) Mistaken; wrong.
The facts are correct, but the conclusion is **erroneous**.

factor
fak´ tər

n. Something that contributes to a result.
Paying attention and studying diligently are two **factors** in getting good grades.

fad
fad

n. Something that is very popular for a short time, then forgotten.
Ankle bracelets were the **fad** one summer.

gripe
grīp

v. 1. To complain.
The children always **gripe** about having to get up early.
2. To annoy or irritate.
Crowded airports **gripe** the traveling public.
n. A complaint.
Squalid living conditions and contaminated drinking water were two of the captives' **gripes**.

knack
nak

n. A special talent or skill; ability to do something easily.
My mother has a **knack** for making friends wherever she goes.

leisure
lē´ zhər

n. Free time not taken up with work.
A sixty-hour work week allows little **leisure**.
leisurely *adj.* Slow; relaxed.
The couple strolled at a **leisurely** pace through the park.

unique
yo͞o nēk´

adj. The only one of its kind.
The platypus, a mammal that lays eggs, is **unique** among animals.

10A Finding Meanings

Choose two phrases to form a sentence that correctly uses a word from Word List 10. Write each sentence on the line provided.

1. (a) A brief is
   (b) an amount by which a number is increased.
   (c) A gripe is
   (d) something that causes annoyance.

2. (a) If something is unique, it is
   (b) the only one of its kind.
   (c) made to last for a long time.
   (d) If something is complicated, it is

3. (a) To anticipate change is
   (b) To effect change is
   (c) to make it happen.
   (d) to be taken by surprise by it.

4. (a) A leisurely statement is one
   (b) that contains a full set of instructions.
   (c) that is incorrect.
   (d) An erroneous statement is one

5. (a) something that contributes to a result.
   (b) A factor is
   (c) a set of instructions.
   (d) A knack is

6. (a) To compete against someone is to
   (b) explain to that person.
   (c) fear that person.
   (d) To brief someone is to

7. (a) that has yet to be tested.
   (b) A complicated plan is one
   (c) An effective plan is one
   (d) that works.

8. (a) time spent away from work.
   (b) Bankruptcy is
   (c) the act of trying to win against others.
   (d) Leisure is

10B Just the Right Word

Improve each of the following sentences by crossing out the bold phrase and replacing it with a word (or a form of the word) from Word List 10.

1. Because of its unusual size and color, this diamond is believed to be **the only one of its kind**.

2. Last year the company was declared **unable to pay its debts and was freed by law from doing so**.

3. Six runners are **taking part and hoping to win** in the 100-meter dash.

4. The machine is **made up of many parts** and will take a long time to assemble.

5. She has a **very special ability** for spotting the problem and fixing it right away.

6. The "pet rock" is a good example of a silly **item that was very popular for a short time**.

7. You **made a mistake** when you said that Thomas Jefferson was our second president.

8. If you **plan the use of your money** carefully, you'll be able to afford a better computer.

9. Keeping your eye on the ball is the main **thing that contributes to success** in tennis.

10. The actors **are looking forward to** a full house for the play's opening night.

11. The drivers **talked very negatively** about the lack of convenient parking spaces.

12. An aide **gave a short explanation to** the reporters about the meeting with the president.

anticipate
bankrupt
brief
brisk
budget
compete
complicate
effect
err
factor
fad
gripe
knack
leisure
unique

10C Applying Meanings

Circle the letter of each correct answer to the questions below. Each question has from one to four correct answers.

1. Which of the following could a person have a **knack** for?
   (a) hard work
   (b) watching television
   (c) selling
   (d) juggling

2. Which of the following is true of a **fad**?
   (a) It's very popular.
   (b) Only a few people know about it.
   (c) It usually doesn't last.
   (d) It usually costs a lot of money.

3. Which of the following would most people consider **leisure** activities?
   (a) playing tennis
   (b) delivering mail
   (c) collecting baseball cards
   (d) treating diseases

4. Which of the following can be **brisk**?
   (a) a breeze in autumn
   (b) a walk around town
   (c) toy sales in December
   (d) a gift from a friend

5. Which of the following have an **effect** on a person's health?
   (a) smoking cigarettes
   (b) overeating
   (c) regular exercise
   (d) proper diet

6. Which of the following could one **budget**?
   (a) one's time
   (b) one's allowance
   (c) one's resources
   (d) one's friends

7. Which of the following can one **anticipate**?
   (a) problems
   (b) future events
   (c) trouble
   (d) past events

8. Which of the following might **bankrupt** a company?
   (a) poor sales
   (b) skillful management
   (c) unsafe products
   (d) mounting debts

10D Word Study

The suffix *-ly* can mean "like" or "in a way that is." (*Brotherly* love is love that is *like* that between brothers.) The same suffix can also mean "happening at certain intervals of time." A *weekly* event is one that tales place every week. At the end of some words, this suffix is written *-ally*.

In the spaces provided, rewrite each of the words below, adding the *-ly* or *-ally* suffix, and write either "like" or "happening" to give the suffix's meaning. If the word does not take the suffix, leave the spaces blank.

Word	Word plus suffix	Suffix meaning
1. realistic	________________	________________
2. annual	________________	________________
3. compete	________________	________________
4. ecstatic	________________	________________
5. month	________________	________________
6. ravenous	________________	________________
7. abundant	________________	________________

8. frugal ______ ______

9. century ______ ______

10. drastic ______ ______

10E Passage

Read the passage below; then complete the exercise that follows.

Fun and Games

Have you ever invented a new game or toy? Lots of people have, and most of them would tell you that it's not all fun and games. In fact, inventing and producing games is a very serious business.

Many of those who have tried to interest a company in their inventions have a common **gripe**: most companies will not consider an idea from someone unknown to them. Companies prefer to deal only with established inventors with whom they have developed a long-term relationship. These veteran inventors have a **knack** for thinking up ideas—lots of them—for new toys and games. Just as important, they are willing to spend the time to develop their ideas. Only then do they take their new game or toy to a company and try to sell it.

Toys and games are big business. People may complain that they have less **leisure** time than they used to, but today they spend far more money on ways to fill this time. Billions of dollars are spent this way in the United States alone each year. Toy stores do a **brisk** business in the weeks between Thanksgiving and the end of the year. They can **anticipate** selling more toys and games in this one period than in the entire rest of the year!

The toy and game business is not casual, either. Companies **compete** to meet the enormous demand by engaging in a perpetual search for new products. These companies aren't interested in warmed-over ideas from previous years; they are looking for something **unique**.

Originality may be the main consideration, but companies must also keep other **factors** in mind when deciding which games or toys to produce. First, the cost of producing a new product is very important; the less **complicated** the toy or game is, the cheaper it will be to make. Companies also take into account the age of the children for whom the toy or game is intended; if it is easy to understand, then younger children will be able to play it, thus increasing the number of likely buyers. Finally, the larger companies with big advertising **budgets** must ask whether they can make an **effective** television commercial for the new product.

Producing a new toy or game is risky, but the rewards can be great. If a company **errs** by putting a lot of money into a new toy or game that fails to sell, the company can go **bankrupt**. If it is successful, on the other hand, everyone is ecstatic. Even success is not without risks. Should a game or toy catch on, the maker may not be in a position to meet the sudden demand. By the time the factory is able to turn out the items, the **fad** may have died down, leaving the company with tens of thousands of items it cannot sell.

In fact, most toys and games do have **brief** lives, but not the all-time champion: Monopoly has been by far the most popular game on the market for decades, and two million sets are sold each year. Of course, only a handful of lucky inventors creates a highly successful new toy or game and becomes millionaires. But inventors are natural optimists. That is why there is no shortage of newcomers eager to break into this high-stakes business.

anticipate
bankrupt
brief
brisk
budget
compete
complicate
effect
err
factor
fad
gripe
knack
leisure
unique

Answer each of the following questions in the form of a sentence. If a question does not contain a vocabulary word from this lesson's word list, use one in your answer. Use each word only once. Questions and answers will then contain all fifteen words (or forms of the words).

1. Why are large companies able to advertise heavily on television?

2. How long do most toys and games remain popular?

3. Why might a toy store owner **gripe** about a severe storm in December?

4. Is the belief that one can get rich by inventing games an **erroneous** one? Why or why not?

5. What is the meaning of **brisk** as it is used in the passage?

6. What happens when more and more companies get into the games business?

7. What are some of the ways you spend your **leisure** time?

8. Why would it be incorrect to call Monopoly a **fad**?

9. What is the meaning of **anticipate** as it is used in the passage?

10. What kind of toy or game usually appeals to very young children?

11. What is the meaning of **effective** as it is used in the passage?

12. Why is the decision to make a new toy not a quick and easy process for a company?

13. What does a person need in order to be a successful games inventor?

14. What is the meaning of **bankrupt** as it is used in the passage?

15. What is the most important thing that games companies look for when considering a game?

FUN & FASCINATING FACTS

Effect is a verb and means "to make happen." It is also a noun and means "a result." *Affect* is a verb and means "to cause a change in." (The airline strike will *affect* our travel plans.) It also means "to pretend to have." (He *affected* a British accent when in England because he didn't want to sound like a foreigner.)

In addition to meaning "something that contributes to a result," **factor** is also a term used in mathematics, where it has two separate but related meanings.

A *factor* is one of two or more numbers that divide a given number without a remainder. 2, 3, and 5 are *factors* of 30, as are 5 and 6, 3 and 10, and 2 and 15.

A *factor* is also the number of times a given number is increased or decreased. A population that goes from two million to six million has increased by a *factor* of 3.

Unique means "the only one of its kind." it is incorrect to say that something is "very unique" or "most unique"; if something is the *only* one of its kind, it cannot be compared to something else.

Lesson 11

Word List

Study the definitions of the words below; then do the exercises for the lesson.

abbreviate
ə brē´ vē āt

v. To shorten by leaving out certain parts.
Main Street can be **abbreviated** to Main St.
abbreviation *n.* (ə brē vē ā´ shən) The result of abbreviating.
Mr. Smith is the accepted **abbreviation** for Mister Smith.

appropriate
ə prō´ prē ət

adj. Suitable or right for the purpose.
Tennis shoes are not **appropriate** footwear for hiking.
v. (ə prō´ prē āt) To set aside for a particular purpose.
Congress **appropriates** money for various programs.

exclude
eks klo͞od´

v. To leave out; to keep from being a part of.
The major leagues **excluded** African American baseball players until 1947.

fanciful
fan´ si fəl

adj. 1. Not based on reason; unrealistic.
One inventor came up with a **fanciful** scheme to turn water into gasoline.
2. Not real; imaginary.
For Halloween the children dressed up as ghosts, goblins, and other **fanciful** creatures.

futile
fyo͞ot´ l

adj. Certain to fail; hopeless or useless.
Before giving up, we made several **futile** attempts to retrieve the car keys that had fallen into the lake.

grudge
gruj

n. A feeling of resentment.
The boycott was organized by people with a **grudge** against the company.
v. To be unwilling to give.
Do you **grudge** me this food when you see how ravenous I am?
grudging *adj.* Done or said with reluctance.
Everyone knew that such a **grudging** apology could not be sincere.

inspire
in spīr´

v. To fill with emotion or great excitement.
Einstein's discoveries **inspired** me to become a scientist.
inspiration *n.* (in spər ā´ shən) The power to affect the mind or the emotions; anything that has this effect.
The sight of leaves falling was the **inspiration** for this poem.

majority
mə jôr´ ə tē

n. 1. The greater number or part; more than half.
The **majority** of teachers at this school live in town.
2. The amount by which one number of votes is greater than another.
The vote was 97 to 91, a **majority** of six.

persevere
pur sə vir´

v. To refuse to give up despite difficulties.
The captives **persevered** in their efforts to escape.
perseverance *n.* Continued efforts in spite of difficulties.
With **perseverance**, spendthrifts can overcome extravagance and stick to a budget.

possess
pə zes´

v. 1. To have or to own.
The children **possess** three pairs of shoes.
2. To get power or control over.
Fear **possessed** them as the car went out of control.
possession *n.* (pə zesh´ ən) 1. The fact of owning or holding.
The will is in the lawyer's **possession**.
2. The thing that is held or owned.
The immigrants arrived with all their **possessions** in a few suitcases.

prejudice
prej´ ə dis

n. An opinion or strong feeling formed without careful thought or regard to the facts.
The critic's **prejudice** against modern painting showed clearly in the review.
v. To cause to have such a feeling.
A worker's casual attire should not **prejudice** a supervisor against him or her.
prejudiced *adj.* Having such a feeling.
One cannot expect a fair verdict from a **prejudiced** judge.

resolute
rez´ ə lo͞ot

adj. Determined not to give in; unyielding.
The shelter was **resolute** about finding good homes for the kittens.

sneer
snēr

v. To look down on with scorn; to mock or insult by words or manner.
The entire audience heard someone **sneer** loudly that the acting was mediocre.
n. A scornful look; a mocking or insulting remark.
I didn't let my companion's **sneers** diminish my enjoyment of the local artists' exhibition.

unanimous
yo͞o nan´ ə məs

adj. Without any disagreement.
The motion passed by a **unanimous** vote of 57 to 0.
unanimity *n.* (yo͞o nə nim´ ə tē) The condition of being unanimous.
The committee voted 12 to 0 in a rare display of **unanimity**.

unruly
un ro͞o´ lē

adj. 1. Badly behaved.
An **unruly** child in a restaurant can be very annoying to the other diners.
2. Hard to control.
This hair spray might help keep your **unruly** hair in place.

11A Finding Meanings

Choose two phrases to form a sentence that correctly uses a word from Word List 11. Write each sentence on the line provided.

1. (a) be without it.
   (b) To appropriate money is to
   (c) To possess money is to
   (d) set it aside for a purpose.

2. (a) An inspiration is
   (b) a mocking or insulting remark.
   (c) A sneer is
   (d) an opinion held without regard to the facts.

3. (a) more than half.
   (b) A majority is
   (c) A prejudice is
   (d) a number that is too large to be counted.

4. (a) who is easily upset.
   (b) who is hard to control.
   (c) An unruly person is one
   (d) A resolute person is one

5. (a) Perseverance is
   (b) the expectation that things will improve.
   (c) Inspiration is
   (d) the power to affect one's emotions.

6. (a) An abbreviation is
   (b) A possession is
   (c) a thought that is shared.
   (d) a thing that is owned.

7. (a) A grudge is
   (b) Unanimity is
   (c) a feeling of resentment.
   (d) a feeling of helplessness.

8. (a) An abbreviation is
   (b) Perseverance is
   (c) a shortened form of a word.
   (d) an incorrectly pronounced word.

9. (a) a lack of caring.
   (b) Unanimity is
   (c) complete agreement.
   (d) Futility is

11B Just the Right Word

Improve each of the following sentences by crossing out the bold phrase and replacing it with a word (or a form of the word) from Word List 11.

1. Greed **got power over** them and led to their downfall.

2. I soon discovered that asking to borrow my parents' car was **a waste of my time**.

3. How do you **write the shortened form of** the word *adjective*?

4. The idea that the stork brings a new baby is **one that does not seem very reasonable**.

5. The decision was **made with everyone in agreement**.

6. Thoughtful people do not let **opinions formed without regard for the facts** affect their judgment.

7. I believe they **parted unwillingly with** the dollar they gave to the Red Cross.

8. The club is for teenagers only, and adults are **not allowed to be members of it**.

9. Only by **a firm refusal to give up** can you hope to succeed.

10. Do not **direct your scornful remarks** at things you don't understand.

11. Teenagers like to wear jeans, but they aren't always **suitable for the occasion**.

12. I think you're making a mistake, but I see you are quite **determined not to change your mind** about going.

13. The thrill of going aloft for the first time **had a great effect on me and caused** me to want to be a pilot.

abbreviate
appropriate
exclude
fanciful
futile
grudge
inspire
majority
persevere
possess
prejudice
resolute
sneer
unanimous
unruly

11C Applying Meanings

Circle the letter of each correct answer to the questions below. Each question has from one to four correct answers.

1. Which of the following can be **possessed**?
   (a) a pair of shoes
   (b) a knack
   (c) a rainbow
   (d) courage

2. Which of the following would be **futile**?
   (a) proving that 1+1= 3
   (b) appealing a verdict
   (c) counting to a million
   (d) boycotting a business

3. Which of the following is a **majority**?
   (a) one-half
   (b) three-quarters
   (c) one-third
   (d) all but one

4. Which of the following groups **exclude** even numbers?
   (a) 1, 3, 5, 7, 9.
   (b) 1, 3, 3, 5, 7, 9.
   (c) 1, 3, 7, 9.
   (d) 1, 2, 3, 4, 5, 6.

5. Which of the following statements show **prejudice**?
   (a) "New Yorkers are rude."
   (b) "People on welfare are lazy."
   (c) "Women are poor drivers."
   (d) "All politicians are crooks."

6. Which of the following are **appropriate** at a funeral?
   (a) antics
   (b) weeping
   (c) flowers
   (d) brawling

7. Which of the following might cause a person to **persevere**?
   (a) laziness
   (b) ambition
   (c) fear
   (d) greed

8. Which of the following would be **unruly** behavior?
   (a) brushing a friend's hair
   (b) reading books
   (c) pulling a friend's hair
   (d) throwing books

11D Word Study

The Greek prefix *mono-* and the Latin prefix *uni-* both mean "one." Match each definition with the correct word chosen from the list. Write each word in the space provided.

unilateral	unicycle	monotone	monologue
unique	monolith	uniform	monorail

1. Attire in which any one person looks like all the rest ________________

2. A train system with just one rail ________________

3. Being the only one of its kind ________________

4. A cycle with just one wheel ________________

5. A dramatic speech given by one person ________________

6. A sound that stays on one note ________________

7. Affecting only one of two or more sides ________________

8. A single large stone, standing alone ________________

11E Passage

Read the passage below; then complete the exercise the follows.

Elizabeth Blackwell, M.D.

In the early 1800s a woman in the United States had few rights. She was not allowed to vote; that would not happen for a hundred years. She was not allowed to own property; if she married, everything she **possessed** became the property of her husband. And if she wanted to work, she soon learned that careers in medicine or law were not considered **appropriate** for women; only men were admitted to medical or law schools. Most people regarded this as a perfectly normal state of affairs. But Elizabeth Blackwell was not one of them.

Born in England in 1821, Blackwell came to America as a young girl with her parents. Later, when she expressed a desire to become a doctor, her parents and friends told her to put aside such **fanciful** ideas because it would be **futile** for her to try to get into medical school. But Blackwell was **resolute** in her determination. She studied medicine privately and began applying to medical schools. Despite one rejection after another, she **persevered**.

One of the places to which she applied was the Geneva Medical School in western New York, now part of Syracuse University. The professors there were just as **prejudiced** as those at other medical schools and were quite ready to reject her application. However, in the belief that a **majority** would be against Blackwell's admission, they decided to let the students vote. Just to be sure, they ruled that a single *no* vote would **exclude** her. To the professors' surprise, the students **unanimously** voted *yes*. Blackwell later found out that they had done it as a joke. That had no effect on the result, however, and the professors **grudgingly** accepted her as a student.

In 1847 Elizabeth Blackwell became the first woman in America to be admitted to medical school. Life in the classroom, however, was uncomfortable for her at first. Some students found it amusing to throw paper darts at her, touch her hair, and make offensive remarks about her in her presence. Blackwell responded to the **sneers** and bullying with a dignified silence, and the **unruly** behavior soon ended, to the relief of the more serious students. Blackwell worked hard, earned the respect of the faculty, and received high marks in all her courses. She graduated at the top of her class on January 23, 1849.

Not only had Blackwell become a Doctor of Medicine with the right to put the **abbreviation** M.D. after her name, she had also entered the history books as the first woman in the United States to do so. Her younger sister Emily followed in Elizabeth's footsteps and also became a doctor. Together they established the New York Infirmary for Women and Children. During the Civil War Blackwell trained nurses to tend the wounded. Most of all, her courage in challenging tradition **inspired** other women and opened up the medical profession to them. By the end of the century, over seven thousand women were practicing medicine in the United States.

abbreviate
appropriate
exclude
fanciful
futile
grudge
inspire
majority
persevere
possess
prejudice
resolute
sneer
unanimous
unruly

Answer each of the following questions in the form of a sentence. If a question does not contain a vocabulary word from this lesson's word list, use one in your answer. Use each word only once. Questions and answers will then contain all fifteen words (or forms of the words).

1. What effect did Blackwell's life and career have on other women?

2. What is the relationship of the letters N.Y.I.W.C. to the New York Infirmary for Women and Children?

3. How much property was a woman required to turn over to her husband when she married?

4. How were women **excluded** from the political process?

5. Why do you think so few women demanded changes in the way they were treated?

6. Why might Blackwell's desire to become a doctor have shocked some people?

7. What is the meaning of **fanciful** as it is used in the passage?

8. How did Blackwell feel when she encountered obstacles to becoming a doctor?

9. Why do you think Blackwell's applications to medical schools were rejected?

10. How was Blackwell's **perseverance** rewarded?

11. What is the meaning of **unruly** as it is used in the passage?

12. Why did the professors insist that the vote on Blackwell's admission be **unanimous**?

13. What is the meaning of **majority** as it is used in the passage?

14. What form did the bullying by the male medical students take?

15. How did the professors' feelings about Blackwell as a student change over time?

FUN & FASCINATING FACTS

Majority takes a plural form of the verb if the emphasis is on individual members. (The *majority* of my friends are planning to go to college when they graduate.) If the emphasis is on the group, *majority* takes a singular form. (The *majority* of the human race is still living in poverty.)

An associated word is *minority*, which means "the lesser number or part; less than half." (Most students take the school bus, but a *minority* walk or ride bicycles to school.)

The Latin verb *judicare* means "to judge." By combining the root from *judicare* with the Latin prefix *pre-*, which means "before," we form the word **prejudice**. To *judge* the merits of a case *before* having all the facts is to show *prejudice*.

Two Latin words, *unus* (one) and *animus* (mind) combine to form the word **unanimous**. When people are *unanimous* about something, they are of *one mind*, which means that they all agree.

Lesson 12

Word List

Study the definitions of the words below; then do the exercises for the lesson.

abandon
ə ban´ dən

v. 1. To give up by leaving in time of danger.
The captain gave the order to **abandon** the ship when it began to sink.
2. To lose or give up completely.
The trapped miners refused to **abandon** hope of rescue.
3. To withdraw help or support from one in need.
The city had to **abandon** its plan for low-income housing because people in the neighborhoods objected.

adversary
ad´ vər ser ē

n. An enemy or opponent.
France and Germany were **adversaries** in two world wars but now enjoy friendly relations.

baffle
baf´ əl

v. To confuse; to prevent from understanding.
Alice was **baffled** by their inappropriate behavior and didn't know how to respond.

blunder
blun´ dər

n. A stupid or careless mistake.
The campaign manager's prejudiced comment was a major **blunder** that cost him his job.
v. 1. To make such a mistake.
The chess champion **blundered** when she failed to protect her knight from her opponent's bishop.
2. To move in a clumsy or careless way.
The Sheriff of Nottingham **blundered** into the trap Robin Hood had set for him.

colossal
kə läs´ əl

adj. Very big; enormous.
The **colossal** size of the Great Wall is what impressed the tourists most.

detect
dē tekt´

v. To discover something not easily noticed.
The witness did not **detect** anything unusual that day.

haul
hôl

v. To pull or carry with effort.
We **haul** the boat out of the water every winter.
n. 1. The amount caught or taken at one time.
The crew was delighted with the large **haul** of fish today.
2. The distance traveled or to be traveled.
It's a long **haul** into town.

overpower
ō vər pou´ ər

v. To get the better of; to defeat.
The thieves **overpowered** the guards and left them tied up in the hall.

rejoice
rē jois´

v. To be very happy.
Family members **rejoiced** when they heard that members of the Mount Everest expedition had returned safely.

scoff
skôf

v. To mock; to ridicule.
People once **scoffed** at the idea of space travel.

sentinel
sen´ ti nəl

n. One who keeps watch or guards a point of entry.
Sentinels were posted to warn of the enemy's approach.

siege
sēj

n. The surrounding of a place in order to force it to surrender.
The **siege** of Leningrad by the German army lasted from 1941 to 1944.

sinister
sin´ is tər

adj. Suggesting or leading to evil or harm.
The villain's **sinister** words, "I'll be back!" sent shivers down our spines.

victor
vik´ tər

n. The winner in a contest or struggle.
The **victors** of the semifinal competition will meet in the finals tomorrow.
victorious *adj.* (vik tôr´ ē əs) Successful in a contest or battle.
The **victorious** debate team was honored at a ceremony attended by the mayor.

woe
wō

n. 1. Deep distress or misery.
The slaves' **woe** was evident as they were led off to captivity.
2. Trouble; misfortune.
The country's **woes** cannot be cured overnight.
woeful *adj.* 1. Full of woe; unhappy.
Those fleeing the country told a **woeful** tale of persecution by its rulers.
2. Very bad; wretched.
The pilot made a **woeful** error in judgment by trying to land in dense fog.

abandon
adversary
baffle
blunder
colossal
detect
haul
overpower
rejoice
scoff
sentinel
siege
sinister
victor
woe

12A Finding Meanings

Choose two phrases to form a sentence that correctly uses a word from Word List 12. Write each sentence on the line provided.

1. (a) A long haul is
   (b) a story that seems to have no end.
   (c) a great distance to be traveled.
   (d) A long siege is

2. (a) give that person one's full support.
   (b) To overpower someone is to
   (c) To abandon someone is to
   (d) reduce that person to a helpless state.

3. (a) someone who opposes one in a struggle or contest.
   (b) someone who assists one in a struggle or contest.
   (c) A victor is
   (d) An adversary is

4. (a) is very serious.
   (b) will not be repeated.
   (c) A sinister error is one that
   (d) A woeful error is one that

5. (a) be filled with happiness.
   (b) To rejoice is to
   (c) To scoff is to
   (d) move in a clumsy way.

6. (a) To abandon someone is to
   (b) withdraw one's support from that person.
   (c) To baffle someone is to
   (d) defeat that person in a contest.

7. (a) To scoff is
   (b) to stand guard.
   (c) To blunder is
   (d) to make a careless mistake.

8. (a) left alone by that person.
   (b) To be detected by someone is to be
   (c) puzzled or confused by that person.
   (d) To be baffled by someone is to be

9. (a) is successful in a contest.
   (b) is taken into captivity.
   (c) A victor is one who
   (d) A sentinel is one who

12B Just the Right Word

Improve each of the following sentences by crossing out the bold phrase and replacing it with a word (or a form of the word) from Word List 12.

1. The robot **made its way clumsily** across the room, knocking over the chairs in its way.

2. The junior team expects to be **successful in the contest** even though no one else expects it to win.

3. We **managed, with considerable effort, to move** the buffet into the dining room.

4. A **person standing guard** must not fall asleep while on duty.

5. People once **thought it ridiculous and laughed** at the idea of women wearing men's attire.

6. The children **gave up completely** their idea of opening a lemonade stand.

7. The Mars landings failed to **find any sign of** life on that planet.

8. The **surrounding of the town in an effort to force it to surrender** lasted eighty days.

9. The **very great** size of the national debt worried the nation's leaders.

10. My tale of **great unhappiness** had my friends almost in tears.

11. There was something **that threatened harm** in the way the stranger swiveled around to look at me.

12. The old bull moose was quickly **reduced to a helpless state** by its hardy rival.

12C Applying Meanings

Circle the letter of each correct answer to the questions below. Each question has from one to four correct answers.

abandon
adversary
baffle
blunder
colossal
detect
haul
overpower
rejoice
scoff
sentinel
siege
sinister
victor
woe

1. Which of the following can be **colossal**?
   (a) a ship
   (b) a whale
   (c) a statue
   (d) a debt

2. Which of the following might make a person **woeful**?
   (a) winning some money
   (b) becoming bankrupt
   (c) aggravating an injury
   (d) being offered sanctuary

3. Which of the following can be **abandoned**?
   (a) a ship
   (b) hope
   (c) a plan
   (d) a friend

4. Which of the following might **baffle** a person?
   (a) a riddle
   (b) a greeting from an old friend
   (c) a math problem
   (d) a clue to a crossword puzzle

5. Which of the following would a **sentinel** be expected to do?
   (a) keep a constant watch
   (b) stay alert
   (c) stay on guard
   (d) set off on an expedition

6. Which of the following might be seen as **sinister**?
   (a) an evil smile
   (b) an unruly child
   (c) a hooded figure
   (d) a casual remark

7. Which of the following could be the object of a **siege**?
   (a) a castle
   (b) a town
   (c) a lake
   (d) a horde

8. Which of the following could be **detected**?
   (a) a slight movement
   (b) the approach of enemy planes
   (c) signs of life
   (d) a change in the wind's direction

12D Word Study

Write a word from this or a previous lesson to complete each sentence. Use the explanation in parentheses to help you.

1. To ____________ someone is to shut out that person. (The word comes from the Latin *claudere*, meaning "to shut.")

2. ____________ refers to the earth's surface features. (The word comes from the Latin *terra*, meaning "earth.")

3. To ____________ something is to give up control over it. (The word comes from the Latin *bandon*, meaning "control.")

4. To be ____________ is to be full of life. (The word comes from the Latin *vita*, meaning "life.")

5. To ____________ something is to make worse. (The word comes from the Latin *gravis*, meaning "heavy.")

6. A(n) ____________ answer is one that is incorrect. (The word comes from the Latin *errare*, meaning "mistake.")

7. A(n) ____________ is a particular area of land. (The word comes from the Latin *terra*, meaning "earth.")

8. To ____________ something is to shorten it. (The word comes from the Latin *brevis*, meaning "short.")

9. Something that is ____________ lasts for just a short time. (The word comes from the Latin *brevis*, meaning "short.")

10. A person who feels danger and gives warning is called a(n) ____________. (The word comes from the Latin *sentire*, meaning "to feel.")

12E Passage

Read the passage below; then complete the exercise the follows.

The Trojan Horse

Many captivating tales have come down to us from ancient Greece. They tell of great heroes, of goddesses and gods, and of stirring adventures. One of the best-known stories concerns the Trojan Horse. It began when Helen, wife of the Greek king Menelaus, was kidnapped and taken to the city of Troy.

The Greeks assembled a mighty fleet and sailed across the Aegean Sea in pursuit. After landing their army near Troy, they began laying **siege** to the city, the home of the Trojans. Although many battles were fought outside the city's thick, high walls, the Trojans kept their **adversaries** at bay, so the Greeks were unable to force their way inside.

The war dragged on for ten long years. Then one day the Trojan **sentinels** saw the Greeks sail away! Further investigation revealed that the Greeks had **abandoned** their camp. The delighted Trojans at once declared the war over and themselves **victorious**. One thing **baffled** them, though. The Greeks had left behind an enormous wooden horse. What was it for? The Trojans finally decided that their enemies had left it as a gift to the gods.

Cassandra, a member of the Trojan royal family, warned the citizens of Troy that the wooden horse was a trick intended to bring about the destruction of their city. The Trojans, however, **scoffed** at her warning. They saw nothing **sinister** in the "gift" left by the Greeks, and they joyfully **hauled** the wooden horse through the gates and into the city. It could not have been otherwise. Some years before, Apollo, one of the gods of Mount Olympus, had fallen in love with Cassandra and had given her the ability to predict the future. But when she failed to return his love, Apollo spitefully declared that when she made a prediction, no one would believe her.

The people of Troy **rejoiced** far into the night. They were too busy enjoying themselves to pay close attention to the **colossal** wooden horse in their midst. They failed to examine it closely enough to **detect** the heavily armed Greek soldiers huddled inside, waiting for the right moment. At last the celebrations came to an end as the Trojans grew sleepy and one by one began to slumber. A stillness fell over the city. All seemed tranquil within Troy's walls.

Then a concealed hatch in the wooden horse opened, and the Greek soldiers emerged, dropping silently to the ground. They quickly **overpowered** the Trojan guards and opened the city gates to admit the rest of the Greek soldiers, who had only pretended to sail away and were now hiding outside. The Trojans paid a terrible price for their **blunder**. Their city was destroyed and many of its people perished; the rest of the **woeful** inhabitants, including Cassandra, were taken into captivity. As for Helen, according to the most popular version of the story, she returned to Greece with Menelaus, and they lived happily ever after.

abandon
adversary
baffle
blunder
colossal
detect
haul
overpower
rejoice
scoff
sentinel
siege
sinister
victor
woe

Answer each of the following questions in the form of a sentence. If a question does not contain a vocabulary word from this lesson's word list, use one in your answer. Use each word only once. Questions and answers will then contain all fifteen words (or forms of the words).

1. Why were the Greeks and the Trojans **adversaries**?

2. What is the meaning of **woeful** as it is used in the passage?

3. What were two ways in which the **siege** could have ended?

4. What is the meaning of **abandoned** as it is used in the passage?

5. What did the Trojans think when they first saw the large wooden horse?

6. What **blunder** did the Trojans make?

7. How were the Greek soldiers able to hide inside the wooden horse?

8. Why was it necessary for the Greeks inside the horse to remain quiet?

9. How might the Trojans have **hauled** the wooden horse into the city?

10. Might the Trojans have seen anything **sinister** if they had looked more closely at the wooden horse?

11. Why did the Trojans **scoff** at Cassandra's warning?

12. What might have happened if the Trojans had **overpowered** the Greek soldiers as they emerged from the wooden horse?

13. Who should have been keeping watch on the wooden horse?

14. Why was the Trojans' **rejoicing** premature?

15. What was the outcome of the Trojan War?

FUN & FASCINATING FACTS

One of the Seven Wonders of the ancient world was a huge statue of the sun god Helios, erected at the entrance of the harbor at Rhodes, one of the Greek islands. The statue was called the Colossus of Rhodes and stood there for about sixty years until it was destroyed by an earthquake in 224 B.C.E.

The word *colossus* came to be applied to anything that is very large. That is why the United States is sometimes called "the *Colossus* of the North" by people of South and Central America. **Colossal** is the adjective form of this word.

The ancient Romans regarded the left side as unlucky. Soothsayers, people who were believed to have the power to foretell the future, looked upon signs that appeared on the left as evidence of misfortune. Since the Latin word for "left" is **sinister**, it is easy to see how the word came to have its present meaning.

Haul and hall are homophones, words that sound alike but have different meanings and spellings. A hall is (1) a large room held for public meeting, (2) a passageway providing access to rooms along it, and (3) an entrance room in a building.

Review for Lessons 9–12

Hidden Message In the boxes provided, write the words from Lessons 9 through 12 that are missing in each of the sentences below. The number following each sentence gives the word list from which the missing word is taken. When the exercise is finished, the shaded boxes will spell some lines from a poem by John Greenleaf Whittier, perhaps the most popular American poet of the nineteenth century.

1. The swimmers stopped for a _____ rest before finishing the workout. (10)
2. The _____ of students at that school go on to college. (11)
3. A larger force should be able to _____ a smaller one. (12)

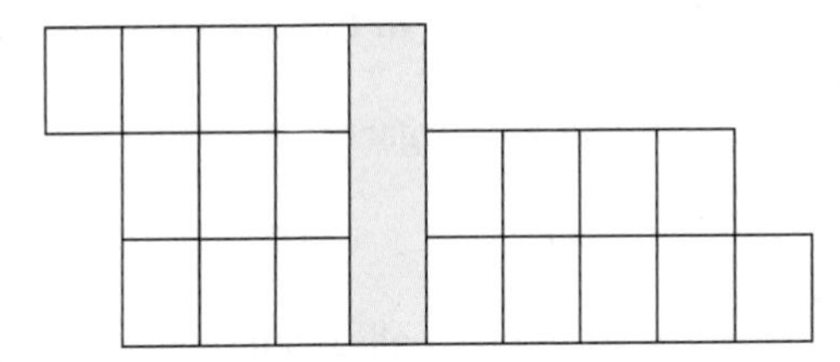

4. All of your friends _____ at your success. (12)
5. Don't _____ at the idea until you hear the details. (12)

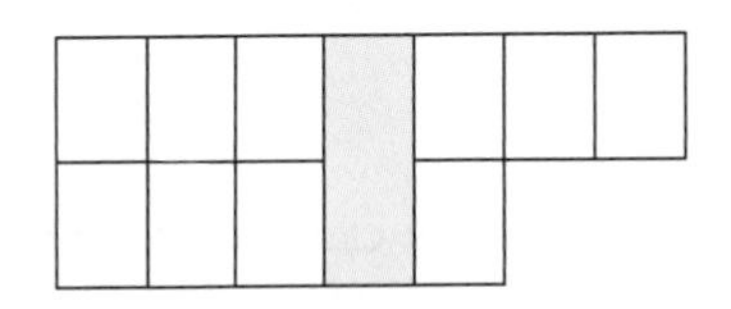

6. I have a _____ of being able to play any instrument. (10)
7. The boycott of the airline may _____ travel plans on this holiday weekend. (10)
8. Their lives were in constant _____ from the rebels' attacks. (9)

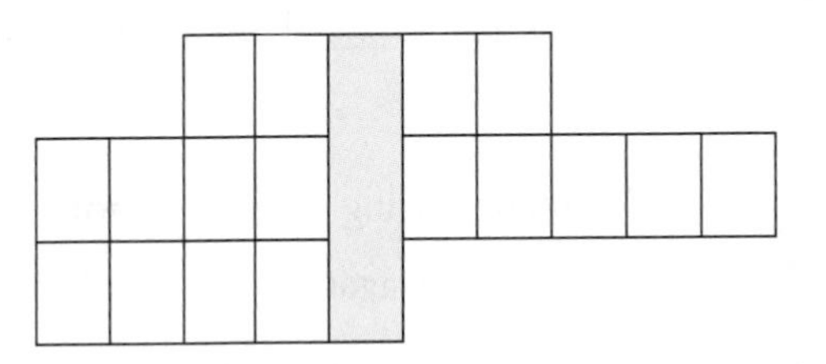

9. The young fan's hopes were crushed when he saw the singer _____ at the gift he offered. (11)
10. You will _____ the injury by not taking care of it. (9)
11. We didn't mean to _____ anyone from the trip, but the car seats only five people. (11)

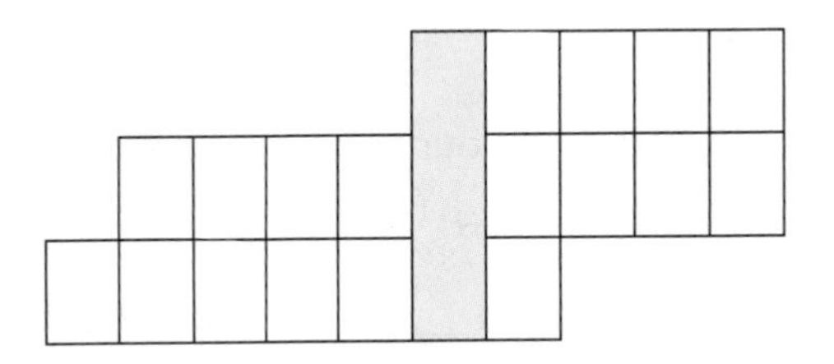

12. Their look of _____ told me they had lost the game. (12)
13. Players who are _____ cannot fail to make the team. (11)
14. The antics of _____ students disrupted the meeting. (11)
15. Not anticipating the likelihood of an oil spill was a serious _____. (12)
16. The governor promised _____ tax cuts. (9)

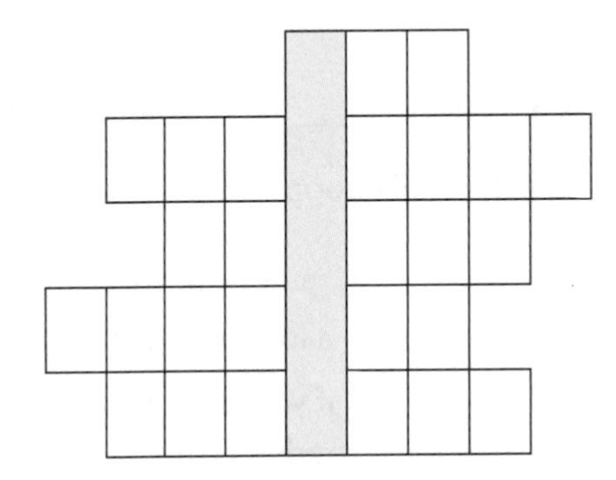

17. I was their only _____ when they needed help. (9)

18. Here's a trick that would _____ even a magician. (12)

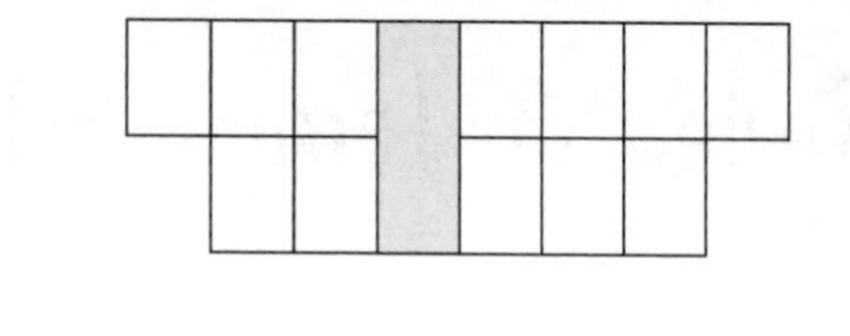

19. The moon causes the _____ motion of the tides. (9)

20. The _____ in the debate receives a gold medal. (12)

21. The kindergarteners' talk of marriage is just a _____ idea. (11)

22. Their _____ is that they don't get paid on time. (10)

23. To say that all people with poor posture are lazy shows _____ . (11)

24. Are you going to _____ in the long jump? (10)

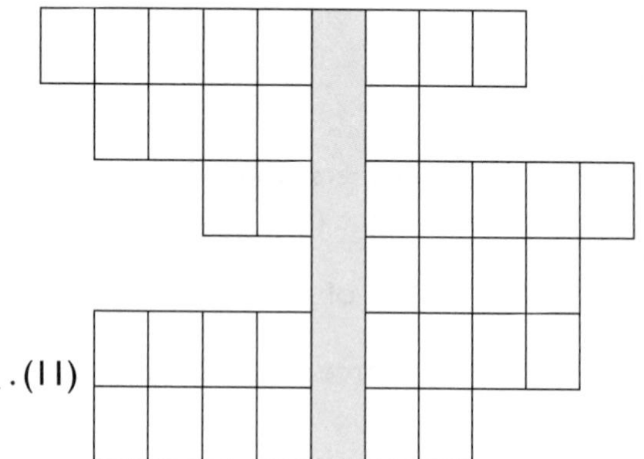

25. A bad back caused Ashley to _____ the goal of being a cheerleader. (12)

26. I do not _____ them any success they have had. (11)

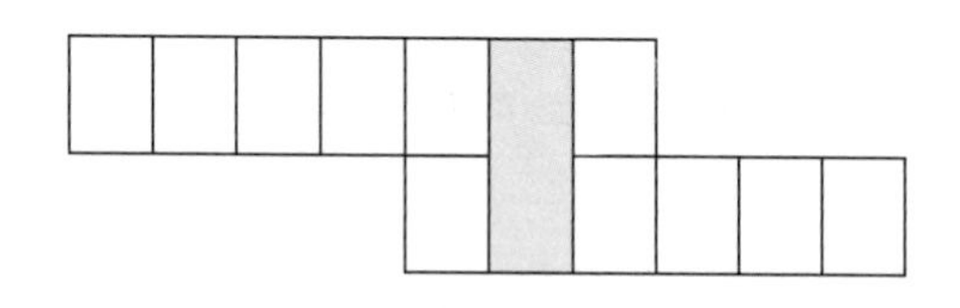

27. Talking during a movie is not _____ behavior. (11)

28. The extravagant member of the budget committee was a powerful _____ . (12)

29. The decision of the five judges was _____ . (11)

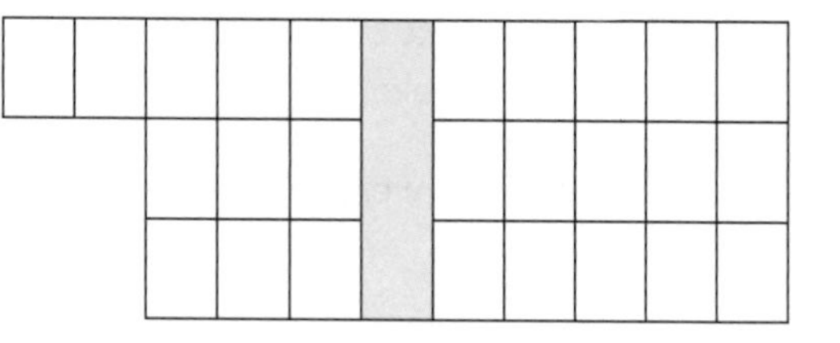

30. Sad to say, our efforts to save the beached whale were _____ . (11)

31. Cracks will _____ the value of old photographs. (9)

32. You can _____ New York City to N.Y.C. (11)

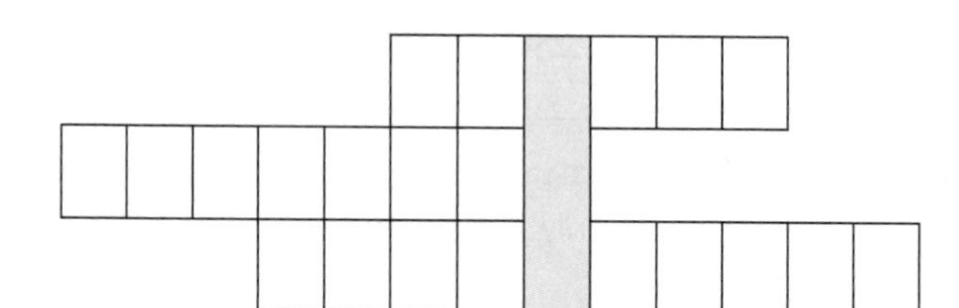

33. Nature _____ Beethoven to write eloquent music. (11)

34. The hula hoop was the greatest _____ of the 1960s. (10)

35. Did I _____ a note of anger in your voice? (12)

36. The _____ allows ten dollars a day for food. (10)

37. You _____ if you think you can attain those goals with mediocre grades. (10)

38. The president does not _____ unlimited power. (11)

39. You can _____ margarine for butter in the recipe. (9)

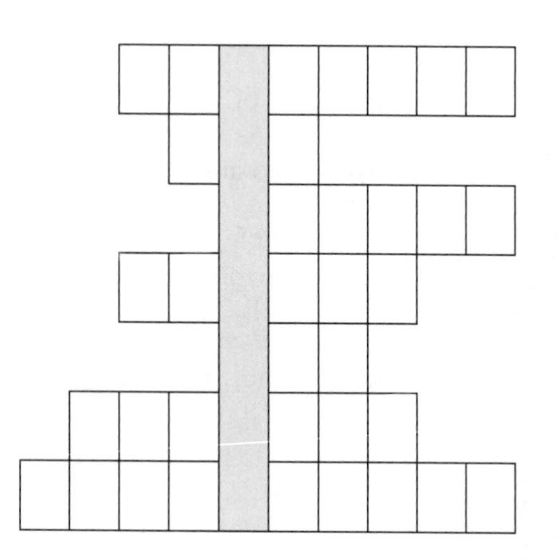

40. The exhausted swimmers could not _____ such a fast pace any longer. (9)

41. Any _____ in the baby food can cause illness. (9)

42. Earth is _____ in its ability to support life. (10)

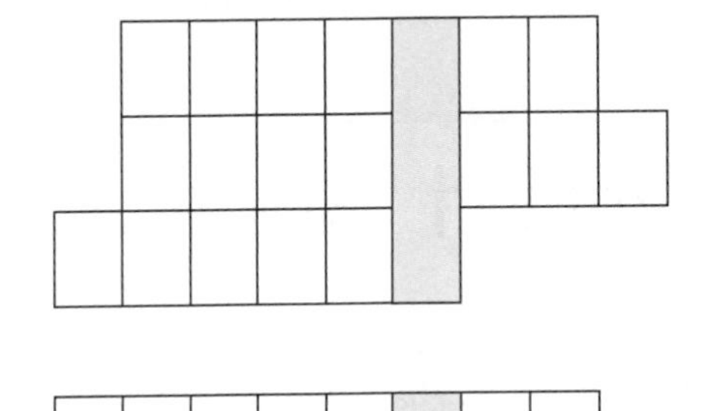

43. The pirate's _____ smile made us shudder. (12)

44. To succeed at auditions, dancers must _____ even when they are exhausted and ravenous. (11)

45. Landing people on Mars will be a _____ undertaking. (12)

46. We _____ energy by moving as little as possible. (9)

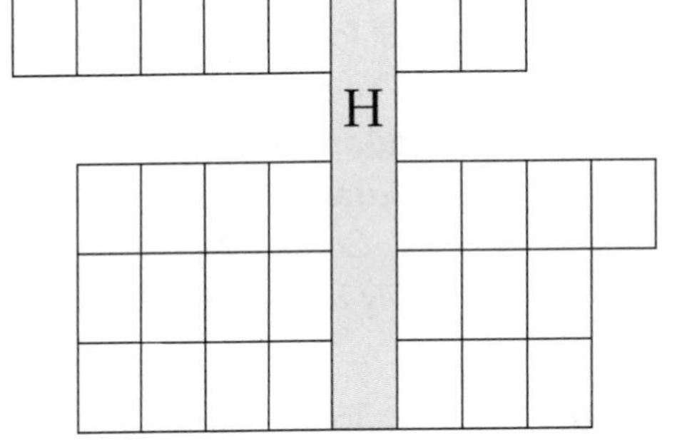

47. Lead from the pipes will _____ the water. (9)

48. Speed was a _____ in the team's success. (10)

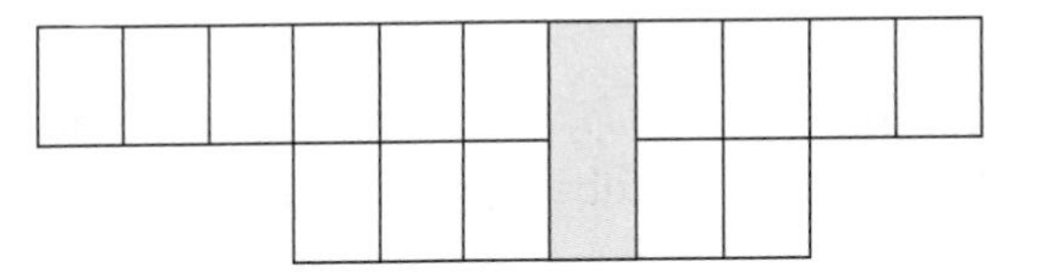

49. Dirt will _____ if the rooms are not cleaned often. (9)

50. I _____ going to camp in July this year. (10)

51. A _____ person throws very little away. (9)

52. The _____ at the gate saw us approach the fort. (12)

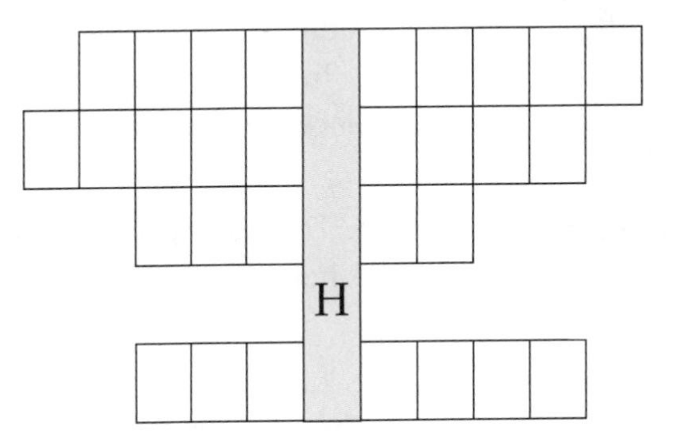

53. A tow truck had to _____ the wrecked car to the dump. (12)

54. It is _____ that all flammable materials be removed from the school. (9)

55. Taking taxis everywhere seems very _____ . (9)

56. Grandfather spends most of his _____ time in the garden. (10)

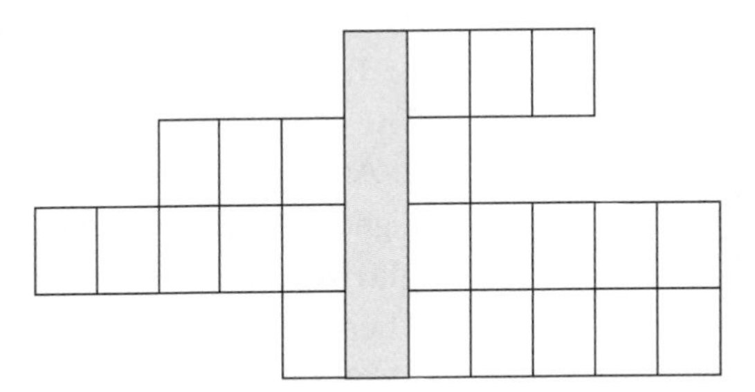

57. Taking a _____ walk every day is beneficial. (10)

58. What _____ does television have on a child's mind? (10)

59. After a ten-month _____ , the city surrendered. (12)

60. The company went _____ when it failed to pay its bills. (10)

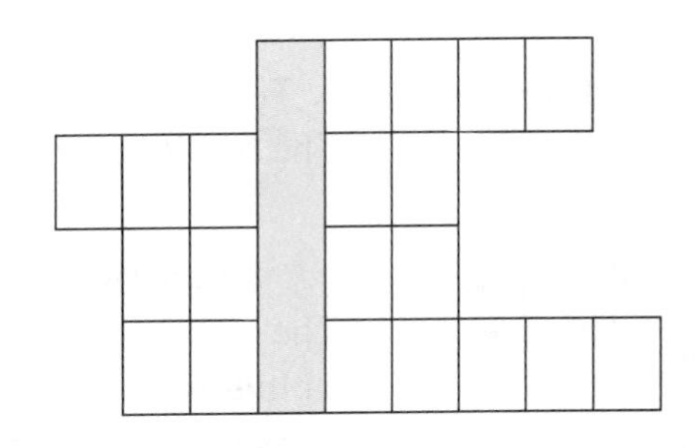

Lesson 13

Word List

Study the definitions of the words below; then do the exercises for the lesson.

adapt
ə dapt´

v. 1. To change to fit new conditions.
Whales were once land animals but **adapted** well to life in the ocean.
2. To make changes in something to make it useful.
The students **adapted** a coat hanger for use as a radio antenna.
adaptation *n.* (ad əp tā´ shən) 1. A changing to fit new conditions.
Adaptation to a full school day takes a while for some first graders.
2. Something that is changed from something else.
My Fair Lady is an **adaptation** of the play *Pygmalion* by George Bernard Shaw.

deplete
dē plēt´

v. To use up.
Unless we are frugal, we will **deplete** our savings by the end of March.

efficient
ə fish´ ənt

adj. Producing results without waste.
Tube lights are more **efficient** than light bulbs.

fatigue
fə tēg´

n. A feeling of tiredness from work or exercise.
Although overcome with **fatigue**, the runner persevered to the finish line.
v. To make or become tired.
Since my illness, even light work **fatigues** me.

gait
gāt

n. The way a person or animal moves on foot.
A horse's **gait** changes as it goes from a walk to a trot.

glare
glâr

v. 1. To shine with a strong, harsh light.
The bright sun **glared** off the icy snowbanks, making it difficult to see.
2. To stare angrily at.
The store manager **glared** at me when I toppled the stack of books.
n. 1. A strong, blinding light.
The **glare** from oncoming cars is diminished if drivers dim their headlights.
2. An angry stare.
I ignored my adversary's **glare**, which I interpreted as an attempt to scare me.
glaring *adj.* 1. Shining with a harsh, brilliant light.
There was no shade from the **glaring** summer sun in the open fields.
2. Very obvious.
The manager detected a **glaring** error in the figures.

habitat
hab´ i tat

n. The place or type of place where a plant or animal is normally found.
The **habitat** of the saguaro cactus is the desert of southwest Arizona.

oblivious
ə bliv´ ē əs

adj. Not aware of.
The audience was **oblivious** to everything except the actor's inspired performance.
oblivion *n.* A state of forgetting or being forgotten.
These tunes sank into **oblivion** after the new Broadway show closed.

outmoded
out mōd´ əd

adj. No longer needed or fashionable.
The coming of the railroad made the stagecoach an **outmoded** way to travel.

prominent
präm´ ə nənt

adj. 1. Projecting; standing out.
Mount Rushmore is a **prominent** feature of the Black Hills in South Dakota.
2. Very easy to see; easily noticed.
Pinocchio's **prominent** nose grew even longer every time he told a lie.
3. Famous; well-known.
The accident victim asked a **prominent** lawyer for advice.

quench
kwench

v. 1. To put out; to extinguish.
Not even reading three books on the subject could **quench** his interest in the mysterious stories about the haunted house.
2. To satisfy with a liquid.
Water **quenches** a thirst better than a sweetened soda drink.

rigor
rig´ ər

n. (often pl.) 1. A condition that makes life difficult.
The orange tree couldn't survive the **rigors** of a Canadian winter.
2. Strictness or severity.
The police chief enforced the law with **rigor**.
rigorous *adj.* 1. Severe; extreme.
The team was put through a **rigorous** exercise program that included a daily eight-mile run.
2. Thorough; complete.
This **rigorous** thirty-day course of study has students speaking Italian effortlessly.

sear
sēr

v. 1. To wither; to dry up.
A long drought, as well as heat, can **sear** grass.
2. To burn the surface of with sudden heat.
Cooks **sear** steak to help retain the juices.

transport
trans pôrt´

v. To carry or move from one place to another.
A large truck **transports** sets and costumes for the company touring with the play.
n. (trans´ port) The act of carrying from one place to another.
The company will arrange for the **transport** of the goods by rail.

wend
wend

v. To travel; to go on one's way.
It took two weeks to **wend** our way over the mountain pass.

13A Finding Meanings

Choose two phrases to form a sentence that correctly uses a word from Word List 13. Write each sentence on the line provided.

1. (a) a state of uncertainty.
   (b) a feeling of tiredness.
   (c) Oblivion is
   (d) Fatigue is

2. (a) A glaring error is one
   (b) to which no one pays attention.
   (c) A rigorous rule is one
   (d) that should be obvious to anyone.

3. (a) a feeling of worry or concern.
   (b) Oblivion is
   (c) Adaptation is
   (d) a total lack of awareness.

4. (a) is in a rundown condition.
   (b) A prominent building is one that
   (c) stands out from those around it.
   (d) An efficient building is one that

5. (a) Transport is
   (b) a change to fit a new condition.
   (c) An adaptation is
   (d) a breaking down of something into its parts.

6. (a) A gait is
   (b) a slight burn.
   (c) an angry stare.
   (d) A glare is

7. (a) To sear something is to
   (b) burn its surface.
   (c) To quench something is to
   (d) store it for later use.

8. (a) An animal's gait is
   (b) its sense of smell.
   (c) An animal's habitat is
   (d) the way it walks.

9. (a) is thorough and complete.
   (b) is carried out carelessly.
   (c) A rigorous test is one that
   (d) An outmoded test is one that

10. (a) a change in manner.
    (b) A habitat is
    (c) the place a plant naturally grows.
    (d) Transport is

adapt
deplete
efficient
fatigue
gait
glare
habitat
oblivious
outmoded
prominent
quench
rigor
sear
transport
wend

13B Just the Right Word

Improve each of the following sentences by crossing out the bold phrase and replacing it with a word (or a form of the word) from Word List 13.

1. If it isn't careful, the state will **completely use up** its oil reserves in the near future.

2. Even a short walk **causes a feeling of tiredness to come over** these feeble patients.

3. Animals that do not **make changes to fit new conditions** fail to survive.

4. The mighty Mississippi **makes its way** slowly to the sea.

5. The Empire State Building is a **well-known and easily spotted** landmark in New York City.

6. **The carrying of goods to where they have to go** is the responsibility of the shipping department.

7. The **harsh and brilliant light** of the welding torch almost blinded me.

8. The lemur's **natural home and the place where it is normally found** is Madagascar.

9. The children can **have a drink to satisfy** their thirst at the water fountain.

10. A tune-up will help an engine be **able to work properly while using less energy**.

11. The method you propose is **no longer in use because a better one has been discovered**.

12. Penguins are well suited to the **harsh conditions** of the Antarctic.

13C Applying Meanings

Circle the letter of each correct answer to the questions below. Each question has from one to four correct answers.

1. Which of the following could be **transported**?
   (a) animals
   (b) terrain
   (c) veterans
   (d) supplies

2. Which of the following is **outmoded**?
   (a) a fashion model
   (b) the nineteenth century
   (c) gaslight
   (d) silent movies

3. Which of the following can be **quenched**?
   (a) a sneer
   (b) a campfire
   (c) thirst
   (d) plans

4. Which of the following could be **adapted**?
   (a) a method
   (b) a baby
   (c) a tool
   (d) a book

5. Which of the following can be **depleted**?
   (a) resources
   (b) savings
   (c) supplies
   (d) debts

6. Which of the following might **glare**?
   (a) a spotlight
   (b) a radio
   (c) an angry person
   (d) light reflected in a mirror

7. Which of the following can be **rigorous**?
   (a) a fitness program
   (b) an inspection
   (c) a climate
   (d) a blunder

8. Which of the following is a **gait**?
   (a) a posture
   (b) a gallop
   (c) a limp
   (d) a haul

adapt
deplete
efficient
fatigue
gait
glare
habitat
oblivious
outmoded
prominent
quench
rigor
sear
transport
wend

13D Word Study

Writers often have to decide which of several words with similar meanings is the best choice to express the exact meaning they wish to give. Write the word from the pair above it that makes the most sense in each sentence.

transport/carry

1. I saw Mom __________ the baby upstairs.

2. A jet was waiting to __________ the important papers to the president.

oblivious/unaware

3. I was __________ of the fact that Mars has an atmosphere.

4. My dog Peyton was happily running around __________ to his surroundings.

woe/misery

5. Cries of __________ came from the people who had watched their houses slide down into the ocean.

6. I was in such __________ that I had to call the dentist about my toothache.

blunder/mistake

7. I made a __________ when I wrote down the address.

8. The candidate's major __________ cost him the election.

peril/danger

9. The child was in __________ of slipping on the ice.

10. The Argonauts faced each new __________ with steadfast courage.

gripe/complain

11. I told the sales clerk that I would __________ to the manager.

12. People __________ at having to stand in line at airports.

conserve/save

13. Buying your ticket through the internet will __________ you time.

14. Modern houses are built to __________ heat and lower fuel costs.

diminish/reduce

15. I will __________ the amount of fat I use in that recipe by one half.

16. The storm did not __________ until after midnight.

captive/prisoner

17. The __________ was released by the rebels after six months.

18. Each __________ in the county jail is awaiting trial.

origin/beginning

19. I turned back to the __________ of the story.

20. Do you know the __________ of the word "boycott?"

13E Passage

Read the passage below; then complete the exercise that follows.

The Ship of the Desert

A long line of camels **wending** its way slowly across the skyline was once a familiar sight in the North African and Arabian deserts. These animals are actually dromedaries, the kind that most people think of when camels are mentioned. The Bedouins, the migrant people of the Arabian and Sahara deserts, call the dromedary "the ship of the desert" because it has **transported** goods and people over some of the most arid regions in the world for thousands of years.

Bearing its burden patiently, and seemingly **oblivious** to hunger and thirst, the dromedary can keep up a steady, plodding **gait**, traveling fifty miles a day for up to five days, without showing signs of **fatigue**. When it reaches water, it **quenches** its thirst by drinking as much as fifteen gallons at a time. When food is not available, it lives on the fat stored in its hump, which is not filled with water as some people think. The dromedary's hump fills out and is quite **prominent** when the animal is well fed; it gets smaller as the fat stored inside is **depleted**.

The dromedary is very well **adapted** to life in the desert. Its broad feet do not sink into soft sand, and it can close its nostrils completely during sandstorms while protecting its eyes with double rows of eyelashes. It is comfortable even in the **searing** heat of the desert and will stretch out in the full **glare** of the noonday sun even though shade may be available. The dromedary is capable of carrying up to six hundred pounds on its back, but it knows its limits. If given too heavy a burden, it will obstinately refuse to budge until the load is lightened.

Closely related to the dromedary is the Bactrian camel, whose **habitat** is the cold desert regions of Siberia, in central Asia. The Bactrian camel is smaller and sturdier than the dromedary, has shorter legs, and is covered with long, shaggy hair to protect it from the **rigorous** Siberian climate. But the most obvious difference between them is the number of humps. The dromedary has a single hump, while the Bactrian camel has two. Although both kinds have been domesticated for thousands of years, the Bactrian camel, unlike its cousin, is still found in the wild.

To the Bedouins and the migrant people of central Asia, the dromedary and Bactrian camel are much more than beasts of burden. Their hair provides wool for making clothes and carpets; their hides can be used to make tents and footwear; they can be milked like cows; and their meat, which tastes like veal or beef, forms an important part of these peoples' diets.

In spite of their great versatility, both kinds of camels are becoming **outmoded** means of transportation in the modern world. Four-wheel-drive vehicles are more **efficient**; they can travel faster and further and carry heavier loads. That long line of camels wending its way across the Arabian desert is joining the American wagon train that headed west in the 1800s—something you see only in the movies.

adapt
deplete
efficient
fatigue
gait
glare
habitat
oblivious
outmoded
prominent
quench
rigor
sear
transport
wend

Answer each of the following questions in the form of a sentence. If a question does not contain a vocabulary word from this lesson's word list, use one in your answer. Use each word only once. Questions and answers will then contain all fifteen words (or forms of the words).

1. Why are camels called beasts of burden?

2. How has the use of camels as beasts of burden been affected by jeeps?

3. Name one way in which four-wheel-drive vehicles are more **efficient** than camels.

4. What is the **habitat** of the dromedary?

5. Why might it be advisable to wear sunglasses in the North African desert?

6. Why can the North African desert at noon be an uncomfortable place for humans?

7. What is the meaning of **adapted** as it is used in the passage?

8. How did the Bedouins once travel across the desert?

9. Why do you think dromedaries do not bother to seek shade?

10. What is the meaning of **prominent** as it is used in the passage?

11. What would a shrunken hump on a dromedary tell you about the animal?

12. What is the meaning of **quenches** as it is used in the passage?

13. What sort of weather might one expect in Siberia's **rigorous** climate?

14. How do dromedaries and Bactrian camels conserve energy while moving?

15. How might a dromedary be affected if made to travel more than fifty miles a day?

FUN & FASCINATING FACTS

Adapt means "to change in order to fit new conditions" or "to make changes in, so as to be of use." *Adopt* means "to choose and take into one's family." (Childless couples often would like to *adopt* a child.) *Adopt* also means "to take and use as one's own." (The English writer Mary Ann Evans *adopted* the name George Eliot because women novelists were not taken seriously in mid-nineteenth-century England.) *Adapt* and *adopt* can be confused because their meanings overlap slightly. It is possible to *adopt* someone else's idea and then *adapt* it so as to improve it or use it for a different purpose.

A **gait** is a manner or way of walking. A person in a hurry may walk with a fast *gait.* A sailor, used to being on a ship, may walk with a rolling *gait.*

A *gate* is a hinged door in a fence or wall. *Gait* and *gate* are homophones.

Don't confuse **oblivious** with *obvious,* which means "easy to see or understand." (The answers to the questions were *obvious* to anyone who had read the book.)

Oblivious takes either *of* or *to* after it. (I was *oblivious* of the danger. The party in power remained *oblivious* to the need for change.)

Fatigue is a French word that comes from the Latin verb *fatigare,* which means "to tire." *Fatigue* has been taken into English with its spelling and pronunciation unchanged.

This word has two other meanings, which are used in the military. *Fatigue* is domestic duty performed by people in the military; *fatigues* are special clothing worn by military personnel while performing these tasks and while in the field.

Lesson 14

Word List

Study the definitions of the words below; then do the exercises for the lesson.

benevolent
bə nev´ ə lənt

adj. Wanting to do good; kind.
A **benevolent** employee paid for the team's Little League uniforms.

consent
kən sent´

v. To agree; to allow to happen.
The judges **consented** to hear the case.
n. Permission; approval.
Students need a parent's **consent** to go on the field trip.

discreet
di skrēt´

adj. Showing care or wisdom in what one says or does.
The committee made **discreet** inquiries into the candidate's past.
discretion *n.* (di skresh´ ən) The ability to handle matters wisely.
The English teacher left the choice of books to our **discretion**.

engross
en grōs´

v. To take up one's complete attention.
The puzzle so **engrossed** me that I lost track of time.
engrossing *adj.* Taking up one's complete attention.
The **engrossing** conversation made everyone oblivious to the ringing doorbell.

esteem
e stēm´

v. To think highly of; to respect.
Historians **esteem** Eleanor Roosevelt for her work on human rights.
n. Respect; high regard.
The players credit their success to the great **esteem** they feel for their coach.
esteemed *adj.* Highly regarded.
An **esteemed** member of the scientific community was the unanimous choice to head the task force on air pollution.

exaggerate
eg zaj´ ər āt

v. To describe something as larger or greater than it really is.
Some donors **exaggerate** the value of their contributions to the campaign.
exaggeration *n.* (eg zaj ər ā´ shən) Something that is **exaggerated**.
Saying that your baseball card collection is worth thousands of dollars is quite an **exaggeration**.

extensive
ek sten´ siv

adj. 1. Covering a large area.
Central Park is an **extensive** green expanse in the middle of Manhattan.
2. Ambitious; far-reaching.
The team made **extensive** preparations for the Himalayan expedition.

fantastic
fan tas´ tik

adj. 1. Almost unbelievable.
The guests on the talk show told a **fantastic** tale of being followed by creatures from outer space.
2. Unusual; odd.
Spectators saw the most **fantastic** costumes at the Mardi Gras parade.

intrigue
in trēg´

v. 1. To fascinate.
The way stage magicians do their tricks **intrigues** me.
2. To plot in a secret way; to scheme.
Benedict Arnold **intrigued** against his own country to help the British.
n. (in´ trēg) A secret plot or scheme.
Mary, Queen of Scots, was beheaded when Elizabeth I learned of her **intrigues** against the throne.

marvel
mär´ vəl

n. A wonderful or amazing thing.
The Amazon River is one of the great **marvels** of nature.
v. To be filled with wonder or amazement.
The world **marveled** at the pictures of astronauts walking on the moon.
marvelous *adj.* 1. Causing wonder; astonishing.
It would be **marvelous** if we made contact with intelligent life elsewhere in the universe.
2. Of the highest quality; splendid.
The school play has a **marvelous** part for a versatile actor.

mission
mish´ ən

n. 1. A special or important task or assignment.
The ambassador's **mission** was to arrange a meeting with the prime minister.
2. A group sent on an important assignment.
The **mission** from Israel agreed to resume the peace talks.

opportunity
äp ər to͞o´ nə tē

n. 1. A time that is right for doing something.
The captives looked for an **opportunity** to escape.
2. A chance for getting ahead.
This job offers plenty of **opportunity** for a diligent young person.

relinquish
rē liŋ´ kwish

v. To let go; to give up.
The little boy who found the lost puppy didn't want to **relinquish** it.

tyrant
tī´ rənt

n. A ruler or person who has complete power and uses it in cruel or unjust ways.
The **tyrant** lived in splendor while his people lived in squalor.
tyranny *n.* (tir´ ə nē) Rule by a tyrant.
Joseph Stalin's **tyranny** over the people of the Soviet Union did not end until his death in 1953.

vanquish
vaŋ´ kwish

v. To defeat utterly and completely; to overcome.
Success quickly **vanquishes** fear.

14A Finding Meanings

Choose two phrases to form a sentence that correctly uses a word from Word List 14. Write each sentence on the line provided.

1. (a) An opportunity is
   (b) an unjust ruler.
   (c) a failure to act in time.
   (d) A tyrant is

___

2. (a) A discreet person is one who
   (b) is kind to others.
   (c) is quick to quarrel with others.
   (d) A benevolent person is one who

3. (a) To esteem someone
   (b) is to be very interesting to that person.
   (c) To intrigue someone
   (d) is to give that person one's total support.

4. (a) a chance to get ahead.
   (b) A mission is
   (c) a chance that is missed.
   (d) An opportunity is

5. (a) be filled with wonder.
   (b) To marvel is to
   (c) To consent is to
   (d) stay longer than intended.

6. (a) An exaggeration is
   (b) a group sent to do a special task.
   (c) A mission is
   (d) a time that is right for doing something.

7. (a) An esteemed friend is one
   (b) who cannot keep a secret.
   (c) who is looked up to.
   (d) A discreet friend is one

8. (a) Extensive claims are those that
   (b) can be easily settled.
   (c) Exaggerated claims are those that
   (d) cover a wide range.

9. (a) is one that goes on for too long.
   (b) is one that sounds very strange.
   (c) A fantastic musical piece
   (d) An engrossing musical piece

14B Just the Right Word

Improve each of the following sentences by crossing out the bold phrase and replacing it with a word (or a form of the word) from Word List 14.

1. The lawyers **think highly of** the judge's opinion in this case.

2. By sheer perseverance we **won a complete victory over** our adversaries.

3. The employees will ask for a raise at the next **time that seems right for doing so**.

4. My parents **gave their permission** when I asked if I could have a pet.

5. The search for the missing plane was **carried out over a large area** but failed to reveal any trace of wreckage.

6. When I said that the fish weighed twenty pounds, I was **claiming it to be much larger than it really was**.

7. The Taj Mahal is one of the **great and wonderful sights** of India.

8. The patient can rely on the doctor's **ability to handle matters wisely**.

9. If you found the conversation so **interesting that it took up your whole attention**, why can you not remember what was said?

10. The campaign manager had to **give up** her claim to a share of the money.

11. The masks worn during the secret ceremony were **so strange as to be almost unbelievable**.

14C Applying Meanings

Circle the letter of each correct answer to the questions below. Each question has from one to four correct answers.

benevolent
consent
discreet
engross
esteem
exaggerate
extensive
fantastic
intrigue
marvel
mission
opportunity
relinquish
tyrant
vanquish

1. Which of the following can be **extensive**?
   (a) resources
   (b) a campaign
   (c) territory
   (d) a puddle

2. Which of the following increase a person's **opportunities**?
   (a) diligence
   (b) bankruptcy
   (c) education
   (d) poverty

3. Which of the following is **benevolent**?
   (a) a sinister look
   (b) a sneering remark
   (c) an affectionate greeting
   (d) an act of persecution

4. Which of the following express **consent**?
   (a) "I guess so."
   (b) "Okay."
   (c) "Not on your life."
   (d) "Maybe."

5. Which of the following can be **vanquished**?
   (a) nervousness (c) jeopardy
   (b) adversaries (d) inhibitions

6. Which of the following are **exaggerations**?
   (a) "This suitcase weighs a ton." (c) "I waited for you for ages."
   (b) "I'll never forget that day." (d) "We almost died laughing."

7. Which of the following could be **discreet**?
   (a) a friend (c) a statement
   (b) an offer (d) an antic

8. Which of the following express **esteem**?
   (a) "You're the greatest." (c) "You're inept."
   (b) "You do mediocre work." (d) "You're extremely versatile."

14D Word Study

Words that have different meanings and different spelling but sound the same are called homophones. Here are five pairs of homophones:

horde	stationary	haul	gait	seer
hoard	stationery	hall	gate	sear

Look at each of the sentences below and decide whether the bolded word is being used correctly. If it is, write "correct" on the line. If it is incorrect, write the correct spelling.

1. There were three exits leading from the **hall**. ______________________

2. Sue closed the **gait** behind her when she entered the garden. ______________________

3. The map showed where the pirates' **hoard** of gold was buried. ______________________

4. The boat returned with a large **haul** of cod. ______________________

5. People **horde** food if they expect shortages. ______________________

6. We picked up the envelopes at the **stationery** store. ______________________

7. The hot coals on the grill quickly **seer** the meat. ______________________

8. Jon's leg injury left him with an awkward **gate**. ______________________

9. A **hoard** of tourists got off the bus in the town center. ______________________

10. The village was ten miles away, a long **haul** on foot. ______________________

11. A horse's **gait** is different from that of a camel. ______________________

12. In ancient Rome, people who wanted to know the future visited a **seer**. ______________________

13. The hot sun will **sear** the plants in those small pots. ______________________

14. The vehicle was **stationary** at the time of the accident. ______________________

15. The price of gasoline remained **stationery** over the summer. ______________________

14E Passage

Read the passage below; then complete the exercise that follows.

The Travels of Marco Polo

One of the most **engrossing** travel books ever written is over seven hundred years old. *The Travels of Marco Polo* tells the story of a young Venetian's adventurous life, and although it was written so long ago, you can probably find a copy of it on the shelves of your local bookstore or library.

Marco Polo was only seventeen when, in the year 1271, he set out from Venice for the Chinese court of Kublai Khan, the ruler of most of Asia. He accompanied members of his family who were in the service of Kublai Khan and who were now returning to China after a visit home. The journey took four years.

The great Mongol empire Kublai Khan ruled had been founded fifty years earlier when his grandfather, Genghis Khan, one of the most feared **tyrants** in history, had **vanquished** most of the other rulers in Asia. Kublai Khan, by contrast, was a wise and **benevolent** ruler. He soon discovered that Marco Polo was an intelligent young man and **discreet** enough to be trusted with information that the emperor hesitated to share with others at the court. Furthermore, since Marco Polo planned to return to Venice later, he was unlikely to **intrigue** against the emperor. For these reasons Kublai Khan trusted Marco Polo to travel **extensively** throughout Asia, carrying out important **missions**.

After seventeen years Marco Polo grew homesick and wished to return to Venice; however, he could not go without the emperor's permission. Kublai Khan held the young man in high **esteem** and had rewarded him with important positions in his court; he was naturally reluctant to **relinquish** the services of such a valued friend and adviser. But finally the emperor gave his **consent**, and in 1295, after a journey that lasted three years, Marco Polo arrived back in Venice.

He soon became very popular because of the stories he told of his travels. Many of his Venetian listeners thought he must be **exaggerating** because the things he claimed to have seen seemed too **fantastic** to be believed. In fact, Marco Polo was telling the truth. He had seen creatures with huge jaws and sharp teeth that could swallow a person whole (crocodiles), black stones that burned with a great heat (coal), and many other **marvels**.

benevolent
consent
discreet
engross
esteem
exaggerate
extensive
fantastic
intrigue
marvel
mission
opportunity
relinquish
tyrant
vanquish

Three years after his return, Marco Polo was taken prisoner in a war against Genoa. The year he spent in captivity gave him the **opportunity** to dictate his travel adventures to a fellow prisoner. The book that resulted became one of the most popular and widely translated works ever written and for hundreds of years has been entertaining readers all over the world.

Answer each of the following questions in the form of a sentence. If a question does not contain a vocabulary word from this lesson's word list, use one in your answer. Use each word only once. Questions and answers will then contain all fifteen words (or forms of the words).

1. Do you think Kublai Khan was **esteemed** by his subjects? Why or why not?

2. How would you describe the size of the territory Kublai Khan ruled?

3. How did Ghengis Khan establish his empire?

4. Why was there no appeal against any of Genghis Khan's rulings?

5. Would it be true to say that Marco Polo traveled all over the world? Why or why not?

6. How did Kublai Khan demonstrate his **benevolence** toward Marco Polo?

7. What was the purpose of Marco Polo's travels through Asia?

8. Was Marco Polo free to return to Venice whenever he chose?

9. How might a less **discreet** person than Marco Polo have behaved at court?

10. What is the meaning of **fantastic** as it is used in the passage?

11. Why would Kublai Khan trust a foreigner like Marco Polo to work for him?

12. Why did Marco Polo want to **relinquish** his position in Kublai Khan's court?

13. What is the meaning of **opportunity** as it is used in the passage?

14. Why did crocodiles and coal seem like **marvels** to the Venetians?

15. Why do you think Marco Polo's book remains in print after 700 years?

FUN & FASCINATING FACTS

It's not uncommon to hear people say, "I had a **fantastic** time," when what they mean is, "I had a wonderful time." Note that *fantastic* has two meanings and neither of them is a synonym for *wonderful*. When a word is misused in this way, its real meaning is weakened. Should little green creatures from outer space take you aboard their space ship, it would be accurate to say that you had a fantastic time since your story would be hard to believe. You probably would not have had a wonderful time, however, since the experience would in likelihood have been a terrifying one.

The antonym of **benevolent** is *malevolent*. A *malevolent* person is someone who wishes to do evil to others.

In Roman times, as indeed throughout history, when sailors headed *toward port* after a long voyage, they could at last look forward to having an **opportunity** to do all the things they had been unable to do while living in cramped fashion on board a small boat. The word *opportunity* suggests this; it is formed from the Latin prefix *ob-*, which means "to" or "toward" (*ob-* changes to *op-* before the letter *p*) and *portum*, which means "a port."

Lesson 15

Word List

Study the definitions of the words below; then do the exercises for the lesson.

analyze
an´ ə līz

v. To break down into separate parts in order to study.
Experts who **analyze** violent crime point to poverty as one of the major causes.
analysis *n.* (ə nal´ ə sis) An examination of the whole in order to examine its various parts.
Chemical **analysis** of the rock showed that it contained uranium.

apprehensive
ap rē hen´ siv

adj. Worried or uneasy about what might happen.
Talk about another war made us **apprehensive**.
apprehension *n.* Worry about what might happen; dread.
The police chief was filled with **apprehension** when an unruly mob formed.

coincide
kō in sīd´

v. 1. To be in the same place or occur at the same time.
Graduation day **coincides** with Akeesha's birthday.
2. To be exactly the same; to agree.
My skills **coincide** with the job description.
coincidence *n.* (kō in´ si dəns) Occurrences that seem to be related but are connected only by chance.
It's just a **coincidence** that the bride and groom have the same last name.

compose
kəm pōz´

v. 1. To make by combining.
Concrete is **composed** of cement, sand, and water.
2. To create or write, as a poem or a song.
The singer and songwriter Paul Simon **composes** music that draws from many cultures.
3. To quiet or calm.
Compose yourself before you get up to speak.

disk
disk

n. Any thin, circular object.
The checkers pieces were plastic **disks**.

envelop
en vel´ əp

v. To hide or cover on all sides.
Darkness **enveloped** the town when the electric power station suddenly shut down.

exist
eg zist´

v. 1. To be real.
Did the lost world of Atlantis really **exist**?
2. To be found; to occur.
Many scientists believe that life must **exist** elsewhere in the universe.
3. To stay alive.
Living things cannot **exist** without water.

extraordinary
ek strôrd´ n er ē

adj. Very unusual; remarkable.
The hockey team's winning an Olympic gold medal was an **extraordinary** achievement.

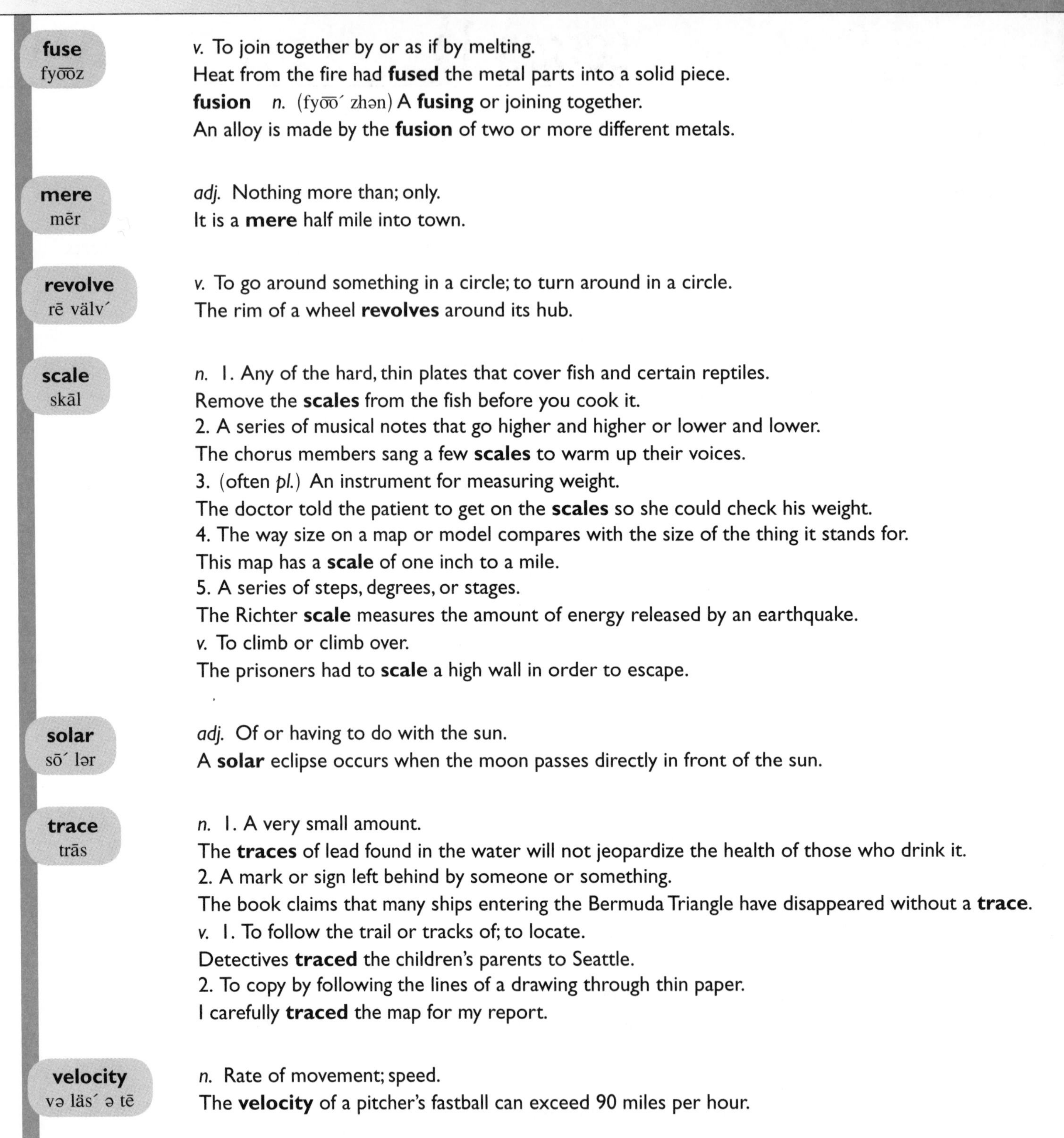

fuse
fyōōz

v. To join together by or as if by melting.
Heat from the fire had **fused** the metal parts into a solid piece.
fusion *n.* (fyōō´ zhən) A **fusing** or joining together.
An alloy is made by the **fusion** of two or more different metals.

mere
mēr

adj. Nothing more than; only.
It is a **mere** half mile into town.

revolve
rē välv´

v. To go around something in a circle; to turn around in a circle.
The rim of a wheel **revolves** around its hub.

scale
skāl

n. 1. Any of the hard, thin plates that cover fish and certain reptiles.
Remove the **scales** from the fish before you cook it.
2. A series of musical notes that go higher and higher or lower and lower.
The chorus members sang a few **scales** to warm up their voices.
3. (often *pl.*) An instrument for measuring weight.
The doctor told the patient to get on the **scales** so she could check his weight.
4. The way size on a map or model compares with the size of the thing it stands for.
This map has a **scale** of one inch to a mile.
5. A series of steps, degrees, or stages.
The Richter **scale** measures the amount of energy released by an earthquake.
v. To climb or climb over.
The prisoners had to **scale** a high wall in order to escape.

solar
sō´ lər

adj. Of or having to do with the sun.
A **solar** eclipse occurs when the moon passes directly in front of the sun.

trace
trās

n. 1. A very small amount.
The **traces** of lead found in the water will not jeopardize the health of those who drink it.
2. A mark or sign left behind by someone or something.
The book claims that many ships entering the Bermuda Triangle have disappeared without a **trace**.
v. 1. To follow the trail or tracks of; to locate.
Detectives **traced** the children's parents to Seattle.
2. To copy by following the lines of a drawing through thin paper.
I carefully **traced** the map for my report.

velocity
və läs´ ə tē

n. Rate of movement; speed.
The **velocity** of a pitcher's fastball can exceed 90 miles per hour.

15A Finding Meanings

Choose two phrases to form a sentence that correctly uses a word from Word List 15. Write each sentence on the line provided.

1. (a) An extraordinary idea is one (c) A mere idea is one
   (b) that one keeps to oneself. (d) that is very unusual.

2. (a) cover it completely. (c) To analyze something is to
   (b) send it through the mail. (d) To envelop something is to

3. (a) To be a mere child is to be (c) nothing more than a child.
   (b) To be a composed child is to be (d) a child in fiction rather than real life.

4. (a) a thin, circular object. (c) A scale is
   (b) a mark left behind by something. (d) A trace is

5. (a) A composed witness is one (c) who does not get upset.
   (b) who is obviously lying. (d) An apprehensive witness is one

6. (a) A disk is (c) A scale is
   (b) a series of musical notes. (d) the highest point.

7. (a) worry about what might happen. (c) sadness over events of the past.
   (b) Apprehension is (d) Fusion is

8. (a) the path of an object in space. (c) any thin, circular object.
   (b) A disk is (d) A coincidence is

9. (a) Analysis is (c) Fusion is
   (b) putting words to music. (d) a breaking down of the whole into its parts.

10. (a) To exist is to (c) To coincide is to
    (b) keep happening over and over. (d) be real rather than imaginary.

15B Just the Right Word

Improve each of the following sentences by crossing out the bold phrase and replacing it with a word (or a form of the word) from Word List 15.

1. I became **worried about what might have happened** when I didn't hear from you.

2. On a **series of steps numbered** from one to ten, the judges rated the performance a seven.

3. Extreme heat and pressure cause the metal plates to **join together as a single sheet**.

4. A microscope revealed **very small amounts** of blood on the murder weapon.

5. The moon **travels in a circular path** around Earth once every 27.3 days.

6. Only a few pairs of condors still **are to be found** in the wild in the United States.

7. Mozart began **creating musical works** when he was five years old.

8. The **energy from the sun striking the** panel on the roof is used to heat the water in the pool.

9. To find the **speed at which something travels**, you need to know distance traveled and time taken.

10. Since our vacations **occurred at the same time**, we decided to go to Puerto Rico together.

analyze
apprehensive
coincide
compose
disk
envelop
exist
extraordinary
fuse
mere
revolve
scale
solar
trace
velocity

15C Applying Meanings

Circle the letter of each correct answer to the questions below. Each question has from one to four correct answers.

1. Which of the following can be **analyzed**?
   (a) rock samples
   (b) the causes of the Vietnam War
   (c) blood
   (d) the length of the day

2. Which of the following could be **traced**?
   (a) the outline of a peninsula
   (b) a family history
   (c) a long lost relative
   (d) a missing letter

3. Which of the following might **revolve**?
   (a) a door
   (b) a stage
   (c) a pedestal
   (d) a tree

4. Which of the following would be **extraordinary**?
   (a) a parrot that talks
   (b) a fish that walks
   (c) a fourteen-year-old college student
   (d) a twenty-foot sandwich

5. Which of the following **exist**?
   (a) tyrants
   (b) unicorns
   (c) feelings
   (d) dinosaurs

6. Which of the following is a **disk**?
   (a) a coin
   (b) a softball
   (c) a dollar bill
   (d) the full moon's appearance

7. Which of the following can be **composed**?
   (a) a dream
   (b) a person
   (c) a reply
   (d) a poem

8. Which of the following could be **scaled**?
   (a) terrain
   (b) a fence
   (c) poverty
   (d) a ladder

15D Word Study

Select the pair of words that most nearly expresses the relationship of the pair of words in capital letters. Circle the letter in front of the pair you choose.

HINT! Look for (1) a greater or lesser degree of the same condition; (2) the relationship of the part to the whole; (3) or the relationship between one part of speech and another.

1. SKIRMISH : BATTLE ::
   (a) trial : verdict
   (b) dispute : brawl
   (c) sword : shield
   (d) lion : tamer

2. APPREHENSIVE : TERRIFIED ::
   (a) possess : relinquish
   (b) tired : hungry
   (c) pleased : ecstatic
   (d) inhibited : bold

3. ERROR : BLUNDER ::
   (a) pain : agony
   (b) woe : tears
   (c) decision : unanimity
   (d) mistake : correction

4. HAPPY : ECSTATIC ::
   (a) joyful : mediocre
   (b) hungry : ravenous
   (c) skilled : inept
   (d) conspicuous : hidden

5. VALUABLE : INVALUABLE ::
   (a) fake : real
   (b) proud : arrogant
   (c) shy : quiet
   (d) soothing : irritating

6. SCALE : FISH ::
   (a) pounds : weight
   (b) feather : bird
   (c) stream : river
   (d) fly : plane

7. COAT : ATTIRE ::
   (a) paint : brush
   (b) shoes : socks
   (c) envelope : stationery
   (d) jacket : pants

8. SOLAR : SUN ::
   (a) bright : star
   (b) cold : ice
   (c) blue : sky
   (d) tyrannical : tyrant

9. BENEVOLENT : BENEVOLENCE ::
   (a) beneficial : benefit
   (b) weary : traveler
   (c) clever : mind
   (d) inept : skill

10. ANALYZE : ANALYSIS ::
   (a) coincide : chance
   (b) exist : creature
   (c) inhibit : inhibition
   (d) measure : velocity

analyze
apprehensive
coincide
compose
disk
envelop
exist
extraordinary
fuse
mere
revolve
scale
solar
trace
velocity

15E Passage

Read the passage below; then complete the exercise that follows.

Our Brightest Star

The sun has always occupied a special place in the human imagination; indeed, in many societies throughout history it was worshiped as a god; the Colossus of Rhodes, one of the Seven Wonders of the world, was a statue of the sun god Helios. People once believed that the sun **revolved** around the earth, which was thought to be the center of the universe. They also believed that eclipses of the sun could cause disasters, perhaps from the **coincidence** of an earthquake or fire with an eclipse.

We now know that both of these beliefs are false. In fact, one of the most **extraordinary** things about the sun is that it is a perfectly ordinary star, no different from billions of other stars scattered throughout the universe. Of course, it is special to us because without its energy, life on Earth could not **exist**. But the only reason Earth receives more heat and light from the sun than from the billions of similar stars is that the sun is so close to us, a **mere** 93 million miles away.

It takes light from the sun, traveling at a **velocity** of 186,000 miles per second, only eight minutes to reach Earth. Light from Proxima Centauri, the next closest star, takes over four years to reach us. If we imagine the sun shrunk to the size of an orange, Earth on this same **scale** would be twenty-six feet from the sun and would be only slightly bigger than the period at the end of this sentence. Proxima Centauri would be over thirteen hundred miles away!

Human beings no longer worship the sun, but they do study it, and eclipses of the sun provide an excellent opportunity for doing this. **Solar** eclipses occur when the moon passes directly in front of the sun and blocks out its direct light. Astronomers eagerly await solar eclipses although they last just a short time. In photographs taken at such times the sun appears as a black **disk** surrounded by tremendous flames leaping from its fiery surface. These flames, which can be photographed only during an eclipse, can reach a height of 120,000 miles, almost half the distance from Earth to the moon.

When scientists **analyzed** light from the sun, they found that the sun is **composed** mostly of hydrogen, a much smaller amount of helium, and **traces** of other elements. The sun's interior is about 150,000 times hotter than boiling water, hot enough that hydrogen atoms **fuse** and become helium atoms, giving off energy as they do so. This energy reaches Earth in many forms; the two we are most familiar with are heat and light.

By comparing the sun to other stars, scientists can estimate the age of the sun, for stars are born, reach middle age, and die. We know that our sun is about five billion years old, which is middle-aged for a star. When it eventually uses up its hydrogen, it will start to die. With no more fuel to burn, it will start to cool, getting larger and larger as it does so. It will finally become so enormous that it will **envelop** the planets closest to it, including our own Earth. However, there is no reason for anyone to be **apprehensive**. It will be five billion years before this happens.

Answer each of the following questions in the form of a sentence. If a question does not contain a vocabulary word from this lesson's word list, use one in your answer. Use each word only once. Questions and answers will then contain all fifteen words (or forms of the words).

1. Why might the sun have made ancient peoples **apprehensive**?

---

2. How might ancient peoples have regarded an eclipse of the sun?

---

3. With which two forms of **solar** energy are we most familiar?

---

4. What is the meaning of **exist** as it is used in the passage?

---

5. What is the relationship of Earth's movement to the sun?

---

6. Why do you think the author says that the sun is a **mere** 93 million miles away?

7. What is the meaning of **traces** as it is used in the passage?

8. How fast does light travel?

9. What happens to hydrogen atoms at very high temperatures?

10. How do scientists know what the sun is made of?

11. What is the meaning of **scale** as it is used in the passage?

12. Is the eruption of a volcano during an eclipse related to the eclipse?

13. How does the moon appear during a total eclipse of the sun?

14. What is the meaning of **composed** as it is used in the passage?

15. How large will the sun get when it starts to expand?

FUN & FASCINATING FACTS

An *envelope* (pronounced *änv ´ə lōp*) is a folded paper cover for a letter. Don't confuse this word with the verb **envelop** (pronounced *en vel´ əp*) which means "to cover completely."

Disk is sometimes spelled *disc*. Both are correct, but *disk* is the more usual spelling.

To **revolve** is to move in a circular path around another object. The moon, for example, takes one month to *revolve* around Earth. To *rotate* is to turn around an axis* or central point. Earth *rotates* once around its axis every twenty-four hours. Confusion arises because these two words are sometimes used interchangeably. A *revolving* door, for example, *rotates* around a central axis.

Three of the many meanings of **scale** have quite different origins. From an Old French word *escale*, meaning "shell," comes the word for the thin, hard plates found on fishes. The Latin word *scala*, meaning "ladder," gives us the verb that means "to climb." And an old Scandinavian word *skal*, meaning "bowl," gives us our word for an instrument for measuring weight. Scales once had two large pans, one for weights and the other for whatever was being weighed.

The adjective **solar** means "having to do with the sun." Adjectives having to do with other heavenly bodies include the following: *lunar*, "having to do with the moon"; *Martian*, "having to do with Mars"; *Venusian*, "having to do with Venus"; and *Jovian*, "having to do with Jupiter."

Both the noun *Jupiter* and the adjective *Jovian* come from the Roman names for the chief god of Mount Olympus; he is sometimes referred to as Jupiter and sometimes as Jove.

* An axis is an imaginary straight line around which an object turns. Earth's axis is an imaginary line joining the North and South Poles.

Lesson 16

Word List

Study the definitions of the words below; then do the exercises for the lesson.

awe
ô

n. A feeling of fear or nervous wonder and respect.
The view of the earth from space filled the astronauts with **awe**.
v. To fill with awe.
The immensity of the whale breaking the surface **awed** the passengers on the boat.
awesome *adj.* Causing feelings of awe.
The herd of stampeding buffalo was an **awesome** sight.

catastrophe
kə tas´ trə fē

n. Something that causes great loss and suffering; a terrible disaster.
The earthquake was a **catastrophe** that claimed thousands of victims.

collide
kə līd´

v. To come together with great force.
The two skaters were injured when they **collided** on the ice.
collision *n.* (kə lizh´ ən) The act of **colliding**.
The **collision** occurred because neither of the drivers was paying attention.

consequence
kän´ sə kwens

n. 1. A result or outcome.
Receiving a scolding was the **consequence** of my rude behavior.
2. Importance.
The matter was of no **consequence** and was soon forgotten.

deceive
dē sēv´

v. To cause to believe something that is not true.
The Wizard of Oz tried to **deceive** Dorothy by pretending to perform real magic.
deceptive *adj.* (dē sep´ tiv) Intended to or likely to **deceive** or mislead.
Watch the mongoose carefully because its harmless appearance is **deceptive**.
deception *n.* (dē sep´ shən) An act of deceiving.
He pretended he knew my son, and it was not until later that I discovered his **deception**.

fatality
fə tal´ ə tē

n. A death resulting from an accident or a disaster.
Fortunately there were no **fatalities** when the train ran off the track.

improvise
im´ prə vīz

v. 1. To compose or perform without preparation.
The actors occasionally **improvise** a scene based on suggestions from the audience.
2. To make do with whatever is on hand.
The survivors **improvised** a tent from bed sheets.

loom
lo͞om

n. A machine or device for weaving cloth.
These blankets were woven on a small hand **loom**.
v. 1. To appear in a sudden and frightening way.
A sinister figure **loomed** out of the darkness, scaring us half to death.
2. To get frighteningly close.
As election day **loomed**, both parties scrambled for votes.

lull
lul

v. To cause to relax.
The sound of the ocean **lulled** us to sleep.
n. A temporary calm or quiet period.
There was usually a **lull** at the restaurant between the end of lunch and the start of the dinner rush.

placid
plas´ id

adj. Calm and peaceful.
The wind suddenly picked up, ruffling the **placid** surface of the lake.

predicament
prē dik´ ə mənt

n. A difficult or trying situation.
Running out of gas at night on a deserted road put the travelers in a **predicament**.

priority
prī ôr´ ə tē

n. The state or condition of being before another in importance or time.
The school board's first **priority** was to raise the students' test scores.

reinforce
rē in fôrs´

v. To increase or strengthen.
Telling frightened children that there is nothing to worry about only **reinforces** their fear.
reinforcements *n.* pl. Extra people such as soldiers or police sent to provide help.
The soldiers were told to hold the fort until **reinforcements** arrived.

stern
sturn

n. The rear part of a boat.
The front of the boat rose out of the water when everyone rushed to the **stern**.
adj. Unpleasantly severe.
The judge's **stern** expression suggested she was about to hand down a heavy sentence.

treacherous
trech´ ər əs

adj. 1. Not to be trusted.
A **treacherous** sentinel let the enemy pass through the gate.
2. Actually dangerous while seeming to be safe.
Hidden rocks make this part of the river **treacherous**.

16A Finding Meanings

Choose two phrases to form a sentence that correctly uses a word from Word List 16. Write each sentence on the line provided.

1. (a) A priority is
 (b) that which causes something.
 (c) A consequence is
 (d) that which is most important.

2. (a) A placid scene is one that
 (b) fills onlookers with fear and wonder.
 (c) An awesome scene is one that
 (d) can be seen only with difficulty.

3. (a) is one that is important.
 (b) An act of deception
 (c) is one that is amusing.
 (d) A matter of consequence

4. (a) To improvise a shelter is to
   (b) make it with whatever is at hand.
   (c) To reinforce a shelter is to
   (d) replace it with something better.

5. (a) A stern reply
   (b) is one that is meant to mislead.
   (c) A deceptive reply
   (d) is one that is meant to soothe.

6. (a) strengthen it.
   (b) To lull an army is to
   (c) vanquish it.
   (d) To reinforce an army is to

7. (a) When things collide, they
   (b) disappear without a trace.
   (c) appear suddenly in a frightening way.
   (d) When things loom, they

8. (a) A placid look is one that
   (b) A stern look is one that
   (c) is very severe.
   (d) shows fear or apprehension.

9. (a) Predicaments are
   (b) deaths resulting from an accident.
   (c) Fatalities are
   (d) results that could not have been foreseen.

16B Just the Right Word

Improve each of the following sentences by crossing out the bold phrase and replacing it with a word (or a form of the word) from Word List 16.

awe
catastrophe
collide
consequence
deceive
fatality
improvise
loom
lull
placid
predicament
priority
reinforce
stern
treacherous

1. The two cars **came together with great force** in the parking lot.

2. Because of icy conditions the roads are **dangerous even though they may look safe**.

3. The sentinels were filled with **a mixture of wonder, respect, and fear** when they saw the size of the approaching army.

4. The police cannot put down the riot without **extra security forces sent to strengthen them**.

5. Because I was apprehensive about riding, I was given a horse that was quite **calm and not easily excited**.

6. Only the pilot's skill prevented a(n) **event that would have caused great suffering and loss of life**.

7. You cannot **say things that aren't true in an effort to fool** me.

8. There was a **brief period of silence** in the discussion while we thought about the question.

9. Think carefully about the **things that will happen as a result** of your action.

10. Receiving invitations for two functions on the same day put me in a **very difficult situation**.

11. The final exams were **getting frighteningly close**, so it was time for serious study.

16C Applying Meanings

Circle the letter of each correct answer to the questions below. Each question has from one to four correct answers.

1. Which of the following could **collide**?
   (a) two stationary objects
   (b) a single stationary object
   (c) two objects in motion
   (d) a single object in motion

2. Which of the following could be made on a **loom**?
   (a) a wool scarf
   (b) a wooden box
   (c) a leather jacket
   (d) a silk scarf

3. Which of the following can be **reinforced**?
   (a) a roof
   (b) a wall
   (c) an army
   (d) a hole

4. Which of the following might **lull** a person?
   (a) a lullaby
   (b) soft music
   (c) gunfire
   (d) a fire alarm

5. Which of the following could be a **catastrophe**?
   (a) a tornado
   (b) a plane crash
   (c) a forest fire
   (d) a funeral

6. Which of the following might be **improvised**?
   (a) a raft
   (b) a fad
   (c) a knack
   (d) a song

7. Which advertising claims sound **deceptive**?
   (a) "Lose ten pounds overnight."
   (b) "Tastes delicious."
   (c) "Win millions of dollars."
   (d) "Look twenty years younger."

8. Which of the following might **awe** a person?
   (a) meeting a famous movie star
   (b) seeing the Grand Canyon
   (c) seeing a commercial on TV
   (d) seeing a space shuttle launch

16D Word Study

Turn each of the nouns below into an adjective by changing or adding the correct suffix.

1. affection ______________________
2. resource ______________________
3. woe ______________________
4. awe ______________________
5. catastrophe ______________________

Turn each of the adjectives below into a noun by changing or adding the correct suffix.

6. splendid ______________________
7. humid ______________________
8. tranquil ______________________
9. discreet ______________________
10. versatile ______________________

awe
catastrophe
collide
consequence
deceive
fatality
improvise
loom
lull
placid
predicament
priority
reinforce
stern
treacherous

16E Passage

Read the passage below; then complete the exercise that follows.

The "Unsinkable" Titanic

On the night of April 14, 1912, in the Atlantic Ocean about 360 miles off the coast of Newfoundland, the *Titanic* blazed with lights as it headed for New York, four days out from England on its very first voyage. Almost nine hundred feet long, it was the biggest passenger ship afloat. Because its steel hull, the main body of the ship, had been **reinforced** with a second hull fitted inside it, the *Titanic* was believed to be unsinkable. This belief **lulled** everyone on board into a false sense of security, which was to have tragic **consequences**.

Although the sea looked **placid** that night, its appearance was **deceptive**. The *Titanic*, in fact, was in **treacherous** waters. In 1912 there was no radar to warn of an approaching object, so when a huge iceberg suddenly **loomed** out of the darkness, there was little time to act. The *Titanic* made a desperate attempt to avoid a **collision**, but it was too late. The ship's right side struck the iceberg, and both its inner and outer hulls were ripped open below the waterline. Water began pouring in, flooding the front of the ship. Since it was 11:40 p.m., many of the passengers were sleeping or getting ready for bed. The slight bump, which was all they felt, caused no alarm.

When Captain Edward Smith received a report of the damage, he knew at once that a **catastrophe** had occurred. He realized that his "unsinkable" ship could stay afloat for little more than an hour or two. Even as he gave the order to abandon ship, he faced a terrible **predicament**: there were not enough lifeboats for everyone on board. Furthermore, there had been no practice drills, and crew members were confused because there were no clear orders from their superiors.

There would have been enough time to **improvise** rafts, but in the panic that followed as passengers and crew were alerted, no attempt was made to do so. Women and children were given **priority** as the crew hastily prepared the lifeboats, but in the confusion many of them were lowered into the water half empty. Fifteen hundred people died that night, and only seven hundred survived. The **fatalities** included the captain, who chose to go down with his ship, and Ida Straus of New York, who is remembered for gallantly refusing a place in one of the lifeboats to stay with her husband.

Those fortunate enough to have escaped in the lifeboats were filled with **awe** as they witnessed the final moments of the *Titanic*. The ship's bow sank first, leaving the **stern** sticking out high above the water. Then its lights suddenly went out, and at 2:20 a.m., less than three hours after striking the iceberg, the great ship slid silently beneath the waves.

Answer each of the following questions in the form of a sentence. If a question does not contain a vocabulary word from this lesson's word list, use one in your answer. Use each word only once. Questions and answers will then contain all fifteen words (or forms of the words).

1. Why is a **collision** with an iceberg unlikely to occur today?

2. Why must the *Titanic* have seemed an **awesome** sight to people who saw it at night from passing ships?

3. What was the purpose of the *Titanic's* inner hull?

4. Why were those on board not apprehensive about possible danger?

5. What is the meaning of **treacherous** as it is used in the passage?

6. How were those keeping watch **deceived** by the sea's appearance that night?

7. What is the meaning of **loom** as it is used in the passage?

8. How serious was the damage caused by the accident?

9. Why might the passengers have remained **placid** when the *Titanic* first struck the iceberg?

10. What was the **predicament** that Captain Smith found himself in?

11. What is the meaning of **improvise** as it is used in the passage?

12. What was the order of passengers leaving the sinking ship?

13. What happened to Ida Straus?

14. Why would passengers who remained on board have tried to go to the rear of the boat?

15. What might have been an important **consequence** of the loss of the *Titanic*?

FUN & FASCINATING FACTS

The Vikings were a warlike people who lived over a thousand years ago in what is now Norway, Denmark, and Sweden. They were superb boat builders and sailors, and they traveled in their famous longboats as far as Greenland and the northern shores of North America. The language they spoke is called Old Norse, and the English words *steer* and **stern** both come from the Old Norse word *stjorn*, which means "to steer." The two words are connected because the *stern* is the rear of a boat, the place from which the vessel is *steered*.

The *stem* is the front end of a ship; it is a wooden or metal part to which the sides of the vessel are attached, rather as leaves are attached to the stem of a plant. To inspect a boat "from stem to stern" is to examine every part of it.

The noun form of the verb **collide** is *collision*. A *collision course* is one that is being followed by moving objects that will result in their colliding unless there is a change of course by either or both. (The small two-seater plane was on a *collision* course with a large jetliner.)

Review for Lessons 13–16

Crossword Puzzle Solve the crossword puzzle below by studying the clues and filling in the answer boxes. Clues followed by a number are definitions of words in Lessons 13 through 16. The number gives the word list in which the answer to the clue appears.

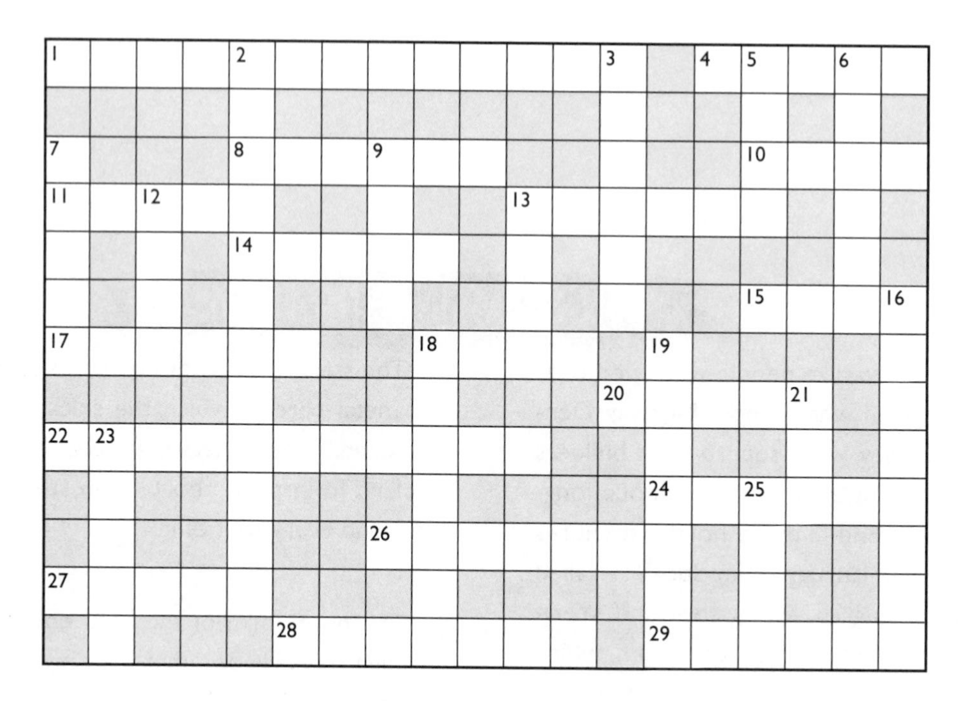

Clues Across

1. Very unusual; remarkable (15)
4. An angry stare (13)
8. Calm and peaceful (16)
10. A machine for weaving cloth (16)
11. A condition that makes life difficult (13)
13. A wonderful or amazing thing (14)
14. To be real rather than imaginary (15)
15. To go on one's way (13)
17. Great respect (14)
18. Any thin, circular object (15)
20. Of, or having to do with, the sun (15)
22. An event that causes great loss and suffering (16)
24. Opposite of *brother*
26. To go around something in a circle (15)
27. "As American as _____ pie"
28. To cause to believe what is untrue (16)
29. A ruler who uses power in a cruel way (14)

Clues Down

2. Worried; uneasy about what might happen (15)
3. Happening once a year
5. To cause to relax (16)
6. To open again
7. A very small amount (15)
9. A synonym for *money*
12. The way a person or animal moves on foot (13)
13. Opposite of *hit*
16. Showing care in what one says or does (14)
18. To use up (13)
19. To agree; to allow to happen (14)
21. Animal similar to but larger than a mouse
23. To change to fit new conditions (13)
25. To wither; to dry up (13)

Lesson 17

Word List

Study the definitions of the words below; then do the exercises for the lesson.

corrode
kə rōd´

v. To eat or wear away by degrees, usually by chemical action.
Exposure to the weather can **corrode** unprotected metal surfaces.
corrosion *n.* (kə rō´ zhən) The process or the result of corroding.
Metal bridges must be painted frequently to prevent **corrosion**.

debris
də brē´

n. 1. Broken, scattered remains.
Debris from buildings damaged by the hurricane littered the streets.
2. Litter; rubbish.
It took city workers all day to clean up the **debris** from the rock concert held in the park.

elated
ē lāt´ əd

adj. Happy and excited; overjoyed.
The **elated** winners jumped up and down.
elation *n.* (ē lā´ shən) A feeling of great joy and excitement.
The news that she had won a Nobel prize was greeted with **elation** by members of her family.

exploit
eks´ ploit

n. A brave or daring act; an adventure.
The spy wrote a book about her **exploits**.
v. (ek sploit´) 1. To make full use of; to utilize.
Windmills **exploit** wind power to produce electricity.
2. To use in a selfish way; to take unfair advantage of.
Unions try to protect workers from employers who might **exploit** them.

leeway
lē´ wā

n. An extra amount of time or space that allows some freedom.
The wide channel gives boats entering the harbor plenty of **leeway**.

miniature
min´ ē ə chər

adj. On a small scale.
A **miniature** railroad for young children ran through the park.
n. 1. A very small copy.
This **miniature** of a 1922 Oldsmobile is only six inches long but is complete in every exterior detail.
2. A small painting, especially a portrait.
The locket holds a **miniature** of the poet's great-grandmother.

mobile
mō´ bəl

n. An artistic structure with parts that move easily.
A **mobile** by Alexander Calder hangs in the National Gallery of Art in Washington, D.C.
adj. Easily moved.
The actors travel with a **mobile** set when the play goes on tour.

onset
än´ set

n. A start or a beginning.
The **onset** of the school year is a time for new clothes and supplies.

ooze
o͞oz

n. Soft, watery mud, as at the bottom of a lake or the sea.
Our feet sank into the **ooze** as we waded across the shallow pond.
v. To leak out slowly.
Sap **oozed** from the deep gash in the trunk of the tree.

pathetic
pə thet´ ik

adj. 1. Causing feelings of pity or sorrow.
The newly arrived refugees told a **pathetic** story of persecution by their tyrannical rulers.
2. Held in low esteem; arousing scorn.
The team's performance so far this season has been **pathetic**.

preliminary
prē lim´ i ner ē

adj. Coming at the beginning; coming before the main event or activity.
The band director made a few **preliminary** remarks before the concert began.

quest
kwest

n. A hunt or search.
The expedition set out on a **quest** for the lost treasure of Montezuma.

restrain
rē strān´

v. To hold back; to keep under control.
The catcher tried to **restrain** the angry batter, but a brawl quickly erupted.
restraint *n.* 1. A holding back or keeping under control.
You showed great **restraint** in not defending yourself when you were unfairly attacked.
2. Something used to control or hold in check.
The child wriggled out of the **restraint** and ran after the ball.

salvage
sal´ vij

v. To save from destruction or loss.
Salvage what you can from the wreckage.
n. Property saved from loss or destruction.
Goods from the burned building were sold off cheaply as **salvage**.

scour
skour

v. 1. To clean by scrubbing hard.
Workers **scoured** the pots and pans until they gleamed.
2. To search thoroughly.
Detectives **scoured** the area but failed to find any clues.

17A Finding Meanings

Choose two phrases to form a sentence that correctly uses a word from Word List 17. Write each sentence on the line provided.

1. (a) To be exploited
   (b) To be elated
   (c) is to be annoyed.
   (d) is to be overjoyed.

---

2. (a) Salvage from a flood
   (b) is property saved from destruction.
   (c) Debris from a flood
   (d) is the soft mud it leaves behind.

---

3. (a) take unfair advantage of that person.
   (b) To restrain someone is to
   (c) save that person from harm or death.
   (d) To exploit someone is to

4. (a) A mobile is
   (b) something that is no longer made.
   (c) A miniature is
   (d) a small model of a larger object.

5. (a) Debris is
   (b) broken remains scattered about.
   (c) Ooze is
   (d) high, thin, scattered clouds.

6. (a) A quest is
   (b) an exact copy done on the same scale.
   (c) A mobile is
   (d) a work of art that moves.

7. (a) sneering at those less fortunate.
   (b) Corrosion is
   (c) Restraint is
   (d) keeping oneself under control.

8. (a) A quest for something is
   (b) a search for it.
   (c) The onset of something is
   (d) a reason for it.

9. (a) a gradual wearing away.
   (b) a thorough cleaning.
   (c) Leeway is
   (d) Corrosion is

10. (a) A pathetic account
    (b) is one that is complete.
    (c) is one that arouses pity.
    (d) A preliminary account

17B Just the Right Word

Improve each of the following sentences by crossing out the bold phrase and replacing it with a word (or a form of the word) from Word List 17.

1. Volunteers agreed to pick up the **garbage scattered on the ground** after the Fourth of July picnic.

2. This is all we managed to **save from destruction** when the house flooded.

3. I saw oil **leaking slowly** from the crack in the pipe.

4. Grandmother's latest **act of daring** was skydiving on her seventieth birthday.

5. These reports are **still in the early stages** and may have to be revised later.

6. The locket contained a **very small picture** of Abigail Adams.

7. "You are **held in very low esteem**," she sneered when she found out he had lied to her.

8. The dog's **harness that is intended to hold it back** is made of heavy nylon straps.

9. At the **first sign** of a cold, I take to my bed and get plenty of rest.

10. We have to be at the airport in an hour, which gives us very little **time to do anything else**.

11. **Thoroughly clean** the pots with steel wool until they shine.

17C Applying Meanings

Circle the letter of each correct answer to the questions below. Each question has from one to four correct answers.

corrode
debris
elated
exploit
leeway
miniature
mobile
onset
ooze
pathetic
preliminary
quest
restrain
salvage
scour

1. Which of the following might **ooze**?
   (a) sap from a tree
   (b) rain from the sky
   (c) oil from an engine
   (d) blood from a wound

2. Which of the following can be **corroded**?
   (a) water
   (b) confidence
   (c) iron
   (d) soil

3. Which of the following would give a person **leeway**?
   (a) extra time
   (b) extra work
   (c) extra space
   (d) extra responsibility

4. In which of the following places might one find **debris**?
   (a) the scene of a train wreck
   (b) a picnic area
   (c) a battlefield
   (d) a tennis court

5. Which of the following can be **mobile**?
   (a) a lamp post
   (b) a telephone
   (c) an army unit
   (d) a home

6. Which of the following might be considered an **exploit**?
   (a) a climb up Mount Everest
   (b) a trip into the city
   (c) a daring rescue attempt
   (d) a serious illness

7. Which of the following might be cause for **elation**?
   (a) obtaining a mediocre test score
   (b) becoming bankrupt
   (c) witnessing a catastrophe
   (d) finding a lost pet

8. Which of the following might be **scoured**?
   (a) a greasy frying pan
   (b) a dusty camera lens
   (c) a dirty floor
   (d) an area being searched

17D Word Study

Each group of four words below contains two words that are either synonyms or antonyms. Circle these two words; then circle the *S* if they are synonyms, the *A* if they are antonyms.

1. final	unique	preliminary	mobile	S	A
2. start	display	ooze	onset	S	A
3. tiny	pathetic	miniature	rigorous	S	A
4. mobile	elated	perpetual	stationary	S	A
5. corrosive	placid	pitiful	pathetic	S	A
6. elation	restraint	joy	surprise	S	A
7. search	leeway	siege	quest	S	A
8. release	exploit	restrain	discover	S	A
9. save	salvage	corrode	collide	S	A
10. use	exploit	arrange	scour	S	A

17E Passage

Read the passage below; then complete the exercise that follows.

Graveyard of the Deep

Ever since that dreadful night in 1912 when the *Titanic* struck an iceberg in the north Atlantic, the great ship lay undisturbed in water too deep for the wreckage to be explored, or so people thought. A scientist named Robert Ballard believed otherwise. He had served aboard a **miniature** three-person submarine named *Alvin* while in the U.S. Navy. The *Titanic* lay in just over 12,000 feet of water and *Alvin* could descend to 13,000 feet, deep enough to reach the *Titanic* with plenty of **leeway**. Ballard's **quest** for the *Titanic* began in 1985 after the U.S. Navy agreed to make *Alvin* available to him.

Although he had an approximate location where the *Titanic* had gone down, Ballard knew he would have to **scour** an area several miles across to have any hope of locating the wreckage. Before he could use *Alvin*, he needed to make a **preliminary** search using video cameras operated by remote control from a surface ship. These **mobile** cameras were mounted on a sled that was dragged along the bottom on a 13,000-foot cable.

Crew members aboard the surface ship studied the pictures from the deep on a television screen. For days it showed nothing but the mud at the bottom of the ocean, and they grew increasingly bored. Then suddenly, pictures of scattered **debris** on the ocean floor appeared. But was it from the *Titanic* or from some other ship? When a large ship's boiler came into view, the crew members were **elated**. They recognized it from photographs and knew they had found the *Titanic*.

Because the **onset** of winter made further operations dangerous, Ballard waited until the following year to resume his search, this time taking *Alvin*. From inside the tiny submarine, Ballard explored the wreck up close. The ship's hull had broken into two parts and landed right side up, almost half a mile apart. Both parts had settled in sixty feet of **ooze** and could never be pulled clear. No one would ever raise the *Titanic*.

Over a two-week period, *Alvin* made a total of eleven descents. Ballard's most anxious moments came during his second dive when he landed on the main deck. The wooden planks that had once covered it had all been eaten away, and there was a chance that the badly **corroded** metal plates would collapse as *Alvin* settled on them. Were they to do so, *Alvin* could become entangled between decks, making a return to the surface impossible and with no way for the crew of the surface ship to attempt a rescue. Those aboard the tiny submarine held their breaths, then let out sighs of relief when they saw that the metal plates had held.

Ballard took many photographs, including one of a pair of empty shoes lying side by side, a **pathetic** reminder of those who died. He made no attempt to **salvage** anything from the wreck, and in a book he later wrote about his **exploit**, he expressed the hope that other expeditions would show similar **restraint**. Sad to say, other explorers did not follow his example. Within a few years, gold coins and other valuable objects from the *Titanic* were being offered for sale to the public. The great ship itself, however, tomb to more than fifteen hundred people, will remain where it is. No one will ever raise the *Titanic* from its watery grave.

corrode
debris
elated
exploit
leeway
miniature
mobile
onset
ooze
pathetic
preliminary
quest
restrain
salvage
scour

Answer each of the following questions in the form of a sentence. If a question does not contain a vocabulary word from this lesson's word list, use one in your answer. Use each word only once. Questions and answers will then contain all fifteen words (or forms of the words).

1. What was the outcome of Ballard's **quest**?

2. What was special about Ballard's **exploit** compared with those who came after him?

3. How would you describe the ocean floor in the area where the *Titanic* sank?

4. What is the meaning of **scour** as it is used in the passage?

5. Why is there very little room aboard *Alvin*?

6. Why did **mobile** cameras have to be used to look for the wreck?

7. What did Ballard have to do before he could begin the main search?

8. How much **leeway** did Ballard have using *Alvin* to reach the wreck?

9. What ended the monotony of the crew members who were studying the television screen?

10. How might those studying the television screen have expressed their **elation** when the large ship's boiler came into view?

11. What effect does seawater have on metal?

12. Why did Ballard not continue his search immediately after finding the wreckage of the *Titanic*?

13. What is the meaning of **restraint** as it is used in the passage?

14. What did later expeditions **salvage** from the *Titanic*?

15. What is the meaning of **pathetic** as it is used in the passage?

FUN & FASCINATING FACTS

Debris is a French word brought unchanged into English. It comes from the French verb *debriser*, "to break into pieces."

The word **miniature** comes from the Latin *miniare*, which means "to color in." Before printing was invented, books were written a page at a time with pens and ink. Pictures in them, usually quite small, were painted by hand. The word *miniature* came to mean "a very small picture." Its meaning was later extended to mean anything very small, especially a small portrait or a small copy or model of a larger object.

Lesson 18

Word List

Study the definitions of the words below; then do the exercises for the lesson.

abroad
ə brôd´

adv. Away from one's own country.
Exaggeration adds to the humor of Mark Twain's accounts of his travels **abroad**.

anguish
aŋ´ gwish

n. Extreme pain of the body or mind.
The captives' **anguish** is expressed eloquently in the poem.
v. To suffer extreme doubts or uncertainties.
Jess **anguished** over whether to tell Bob that she had seen him cheating.

commence
kə mens´

v. To start; to begin.
The school year **commences** on September 9.

commend
kə mend´

v. 1. To speak of with approval; to praise.
The teacher **commended** the students who excelled on the test.
2. To put in the care of.
A burial at sea usually ends with the words, "We **commend** this body to the deep."

controversy
kän´ trə vʉr sē

n. A public dispute that arouses strong feelings.
The plan to build a new power station in an unspoiled rural area created **controversy**.
controversial *adj.* (kän trə vʉr´ shəl) Causing controversy.
The school board's **controversial** decision to extend the school year was approved by a majority of one.

cordial
kôr´ jəl

adj. Sincerely warm and friendly.
The guests received a **cordial** welcome at the studio.

dissent
di sent´

v. To disagree.
Only one senator **dissented** when the vote was taken.
n. The expression of a difference of opinion.
Dissent in a tyrannical government is often punished severely.

earnest
ʉr nəst´

adj. Serious and important; not light and playful.
The victim's **earnest** appeal for help could not be ignored.

elicit
ē lis´ it

v. To draw out or to cause.
The fiery speech **elicited** an angry response from the crowd.

exhilaration
eg zil ə rā´ shən

n. Excitement; a state of elation.
The baseball fans showed their **exhilaration** by running onto the field and carrying the players off shoulder high.
exhilarating *adj.* (eg zil´ ə rāt iŋ) Exciting; stimulating.
The high point of our day at the fair was the **exhilarating** ride on the roller coaster.
exhilarate *v.* (eg zil´ ə rāt) To excite; to cause to feel lively.
The sound of a big brass band never fails to **exhilarate** the crowds.

genuine
jen´ yo͞o in

adj. 1. Real; being what it seems to be.
This is a **genuine** diamond, not a fake.
2. Honest; sincere.
As a result of the successful boycott, the company made a **genuine** effort to stop polluting the ground water.

hoax
hōks

n. An act intended to fool or deceive others.
We knew the player's injury was a **hoax** when he jumped to his feet and laughed at us.
v. To fool; to play a trick on.
Alisha believed she had won first prize until she learned that her friends had **hoaxed** her.

manipulate
mə nip´ yo͞o lāt

v. 1. To operate using the hands, especially in a skillful way.
The deft players **manipulated** the controls of the video game with incredible speed.
2. To control in a secret or unfair way.
Real friends don't **manipulate** each other into doing things that feel wrong.

recount
rē kount´

v. To give a detailed account of.
The judge asked the witness to **recount** what happened just before the accident.
n. (rē´ kount) A second count, as of the vote in an election.
The candidate who lost by only three votes immediately demanded a **recount**.

skeptic
skep´ tik

n. A person who is not easy to convince unless positive proof is offered.
When it comes to astrology, my cousin remains a **skeptic**.
skeptical *adj.* Showing doubt or an unwillingness to believe.
I gave the inept dancer a **skeptical** look when he offered to teach me to tango.
skepticism *n.* (skep´ tə siz əm) An attitude of doubt or disbelief.
The statement that the test didn't really matter was greeted with **skepticism**.

18A Finding Meanings

Choose two phrases to form a sentence that correctly uses a word from Word List 18. Write each sentence on the line provided.

1. (a) To commend someone is to
   (b) play a trick on that person.
   (c) criticize that person.
   (d) To hoax someone is to

2. (a) A skeptical response is one that
   (b) A cordial response is one that
   (c) is very friendly.
   (d) is difficult to figure out.

3. (a) that does not require a reply.
   (b) that is deeply felt.
   (c) An earnest request is one
   (d) A controversial request is one

4. (a) To be exhilarated is to
   (b) be in a bad mood.
   (c) To be abroad is to
   (d) be away from one's country.

5. (a) Dissent is
   (b) encouragement to do better or try harder.
   (c) Anguish is
   (d) the expression of strong disagreement.

6. (a) If something is controversial,
   (b) it is not a fake.
   (c) If something is genuine,
   (d) it is of very little value.

7. (a) operate it by hand.
   (b) To recount something is to
   (c) break it down into its separate parts.
   (d) To manipulate something is to

8. (a) To commence something is to
   (b) To elicit something is to
   (c) bring it to an end.
   (d) get started on it.

9. (a) one who shows doubt or disbelief.
   (b) A skeptic is
   (c) one in a state of extreme joy.
   (d) An anguished person is

10. (a) deny that it occurred.
    (b) To recount something is to
    (c) put it in someone's care.
    (d) To commend something is to

18B Just the Right Word

Improve each of the following sentences by crossing out the bold phrase and replacing it with a word (or a form of the word) from Word List 18.

1. The decision to reduce the size of the police force was certainly the cause of a **public dispute that aroused very strong feelings on both sides of the issue**.

2. We didn't detect that we were being **secretly controlled in an unfair way** by those in power.

3. The candidate won by such a large majority that there was no need for a **second count of the votes**.

4. Since no one **expressed any disagreement**, the decision was unanimous.

5. The students' visit to Paris was their first trip **away from their own country**.

6. The mayor **spoke very highly of** the workers who contributed to the anti-litter campaign.

7. White-water rafting was a(n) **extremely exciting** experience.

8. By making a(n) **honest and sincere** effort you have won my support.

9. My older sister **suffered extreme doubts and uncertainties** over whether to join the Navy or go to college.

10. Banging on the door failed to **bring about** any response from inside.

11. The story that tomorrow's classes had been canceled turned out to be a **trick intended to deceive people**.

18C Applying Meanings

Circle the letter of each correct answer to the questions below. Each question has from one to four correct answers.

abroad
anguish
commence
commend
controversy
cordial
dissent
earnest
elicit
exhilaration
genuine
hoax
manipulate
recount
skeptic

1. Which of the following could cause **anguish**?
   (a) awaiting a verdict
   (b) being kidnapped
   (c) facing bankruptcy
   (d) suffering fatigue

2. Which of the following might cause **controversy**?
   (a) closing a school
   (b) firing a police chief
   (c) abolishing the death penalty
   (d) refusing to eat spinach

3. Which of the following could **exhilarate** a person?
   (a) catching a cold
   (b) triumphing over an adversary
   (c) skydiving
   (d) hitting a home run

4. Which of the following might be easily **manipulated**?
   (a) a skeptical person
   (b) a baffled person
   (c) a person in awe
   (d) a very young person

5. Which of the following can be **elicited**?
   (a) a response
   (b) an explanation
   (c) a reply
   (d) an offer

6. About which of the following statements might one be **skeptical**?
   (a) "Danger—no swimming!"
   (b) "Smoking can't hurt you."
   (c) "Learn to speak Greek in ten days!"
   (d) "You don't need to study."

7. Which of the following could be **recounted**?
   (a) an exciting adventure
   (b) a day's activities
   (c) votes in a close election
   (d) the letters of the alphabet

8. From which of the following could a person **dissent**?
   (a) a unanimous decision
   (b) a prejudiced opinion
   (c) an awkward predicament
   (d) a preliminary finding

18D Word Study

Write a word from this or a previous lesson to complete each sentence. Use the explanation in parentheses to help you.

1. A(n) ______________________ feature is one that sticks out from what is around it. (The word comes from the Latin *minere*, meaning "to stick out.")

2. A(n) ______________________ is an area occupied by certain plants and animals. (The word comes from the Latin *habitare*, meaning "to occupy.")

3. To ______________________ is to operate with the hands. (The word comes from the Latin *manus*, meaning "hand.")

4. To be ______________________ is to be happy and excited. (The word comes from the Latin *hilarus*, meaning "cheerful.")

5. ______________________ is a state of forgetting. (The word comes from the Latin *oblivisci*, meaning "to forget.")

6. To ______________________ is to plot in a secret or underhanded way. (The word comes from the Latin *intricare*, meaning "tangle.")

7. A(n) ______________________ person is one who wishes the best for others. (The word comes from the Latin *volens*, meaning "wishing.")

8. To be ______________________ is to be gripped by fear or nervousness. (The word comes from the Latin *prehendar* meaning "to grip.")

9. A(n) ________________________ greeting is one that is heartfelt and warm. (The word comes from the Latin *cord*, meaning "heart.")

10. To ________________________ goods is to carry them from one place to another. (The word comes from the Latin *portare*, meaning "to carry.")

18E Passage

Read the passage below; then complete the exercise that follows.

Journey to the Soviet Union

Writing a letter to a famous person, especially if it **elicits** a reply, can be very satisfying. Samantha Smith found this to be true in 1983 after she wrote a letter to the head of the Soviet Union. Although she was only in the fifth grade, Samantha was interested in world affairs, and she **anguished** over the possibility of a nuclear war between the United States and the Soviet Union. Her letter contained an **earnest** plea for the two superpowers to settle their differences without war.

Six months after mailing the letter, Samantha received a mysterious phone call. A man speaking with a strong Russian accent thanked her for her letter and told her she would be receiving a written reply within a few days. Samantha was not sure that the phone call was **genuine**; she thought that it might be a **hoax** by one of her father's friends. Although her father denied it, Samantha remained **skeptical**. Her doubts were ended, however, when an envelope from the Soviet embassy in Washington was delivered to her home in Maine. Inside it was a **cordial** letter from Yuri Andropov, the Soviet leader, thanking her for taking the trouble to write and expressing a concern similar to her own about the threat of nuclear war. It also included an invitation to Samantha and her parents to visit the Soviet Union.

Samantha found herself famous overnight. She appeared on national television and was written about in magazines. Not everyone agreed that her visit to the Soviet Union would be desirable, however, and people nationwide were soon discussing the issue. Those who supported her **commended** her for what she was doing and praised her as an example to young people everywhere. Those who **dissented** from this view believed that she should decline the invitation and stay home; they thought that she was being **manipulated** by the Communists, who would use her visit for their own purposes. Samantha ignored the **controversy** swirling about her, and in July, 1983, accompanied by her parents, she went to the Soviet Union.

She had never been **abroad** before, and she found the experience **exhilarating**. On her return she wrote a book called *Journey to the Soviet Union* in which she **recounts** everything that happened during her visit. She was also invited to co-star in a television series. Her life at that point must have seemed like a fairy tale, and all because of a letter she had written.

With the collapse of communism in the Soviet Union in 1991, the threat of nuclear war was greatly reduced. Unfortunately, Samantha did not live to see it. In 1985, shortly after she had **commenced** filming the new television series, she and her father died in a plane crash. Yet, in her short life she accomplished a great deal. She showed that if a young person, even one in elementary school, is willing to make her voice heard, the world will sometimes listen.

abroad
anguish
commence
commend
controversy
cordial
dissent
earnest
elicit
exhilaration
genuine
hoax
manipulate
recount
skeptic

Answer each of the following questions in the form of a sentence. If a question does not contain a vocabulary word from this lesson's word list, use one in your answer. Use each word only once. Questions and answers will then contain all fifteen words (or forms of the words).

1. What made Samantha's visit to the Soviet Union special?

2. How does the passage make clear that Samantha was a concerned citizen?

3. Do you think Samantha is to be **commended** for writing the letter? Why or why not?

4. Why do you think the Soviet leaders took Samantha's letter seriously?

5. What does Samantha's show of **skepticism** tell you about her?

6. What is the meaning of **genuine** as it is used in the passage?

7. When did Samantha realize that the phone call she had received was not a **hoax**?

8. What kind of response to her letter did Samantha receive?

9. Why did Samantha's letter **elicit** so much attention?

10. Why was Samantha's planned trip **controversial**?

11. What is the meaning of **manipulated** as it is used in the passage?

12. Did everyone agree that Samantha's trip to the Soviet Union was a good idea?

13. When did Samantha's trip to the Soviet Union **commence**?

14. What is the meaning of **recounts** as it is used in the passage?

15. How do you think Samantha must have felt about appearing in a television series?

FUN & FASCINATING FACTS

The Latin word for "heart" is *cor* and forms the root of the adjective **cordial**. The heart was once believed to be the place where the emotions were located, and this is still reflected in our language. If someone speaks "from the heart," that person is being honest and sincere. Similarly, a *cordial* greeting is one that is *heart*warming.

The antonym of **dissent** is *assent*. To *dissent* from a decision that is made is to express one's disagreement with it. To *assent* to a decision is to agree with it and to voice one's approval.

Don't confuse the verb **elicit**, which means "to draw out" or "to cause," with the adjective **illicit**, which means "illegal" or "forbidden." (A person selling illegal goods is engaging in an *illicit* activity.)

Lesson 19

Word List

Study the definitions of the words below; then do the exercises for the lesson.

breach
brēch

n. 1. An opening made by battering.
Water poured through the **breach** in the dam.
2. A breaking or being broken.
Your attempts to manipulate your roommate are what caused the **breach** in your friendship.
v. 1. To break through.
The eager spectators **breached** the barriers along the parade route.
2. To fail to keep; to break.
Not making payments on time **breaches** the agreement you made.

clammy
klam´ ē

adj. Cold and damp.
The speaker was so nervous his hands were **clammy** with sweat.

construct
kən struckt´

v. To build; to make by fitting the parts together.
We **constructed** the tree house from pieces of scrap lumber.
construction *n.* (kən struk´ shən) 1.The act of building.
The mason salvaged used bricks for the **construction** of the walk.
2. Something that is built.
The Great Pyramid is an extraordinary **construction**.

elaborate
ē lab´ ə rət

adj. Having great detail; done with much care.
The **elaborate** meal took hours to prepare.
v. (ē lab´ ə rāt) To give more details.
Could you **elaborate** on the plan so that the contributors can get a better understanding of it?

fragrant
frā´ grənt

adj. Having a pleasant smell.
We awoke to the **fragrant** aroma of freshly baked bread.
fragrance *n.* A sweet or pleasant smell.
The **fragrance** of her perfume lingered after she had departed.

furnish
fur´ nish

v. 1. To equip with what is needed; to supply.
The parents' club **furnished** most of the money for the art project.
2. To put furniture into.
The children **furnished** their room with bunk beds and matching dressers.
furnishings *n.* pl. Articles of furniture for the home or office.
Most of the **furnishings** in my grandparents' house are genuine antiques.

haven
hā´ vən

n. A place of safety; a sanctuary.
The local school was a **haven** for those made homeless by the hurricane.

install
in stôl´

v. 1. To put in place or set up.
We want to **install** a large skylight over the kitchen sink.
2. To place into office.
The members will **install** their new president at the next meeting.

massive
mas´ iv

adj. Very large and solid; heavy.
A **massive** meteorite collided with the Mexican coast 65 million years ago, making a crater nearly 200 miles across.

repel
rē pel´

v. 1. To drive away.
To **repel** mosquitoes, use this spray before going out in the woods.
2. To throw off; to shed.
A good raincoat is treated to **repel** water.
3. To disgust.
Cruelty to animals **repels** me.
repellent *n.* Something that repels.
This **repellent** is supposed to keep cats off the furniture.
adj. 1. Able to repel.
My slicker is both water **repellent** and warm.
2. Disgusting.
The way movies glorify violence is **repellent** to many Americans.

restore
rē stôr´

v. 1. To give back.
The police **restored** the stolen goods to the rightful owners.
2. To bring back to the original condition.
A good polishing will **restore** the shine to the brass candlesticks.
restoration *n.* (res tər ā´ shən) 1. The bringing back to the original condition.
The Mount Vernon Ladies Association began the **restoration** of George and Martha Washington's home in 1858.
2. The thing that is brought back to its original state.
Many of the buildings at Williamsburg are **restorations** from colonial America.

retaliate
rē tal´ ē āt

v. To return an injury, usually in the same way.
When my friend hid my bat, I **retaliated** by hiding her softball mitt.
retaliation *n.* (rē tal ē ā´ shən) The act of retaliating.
Should a local warlord attack UN peacekeeping troops, **retaliation** will be swift and certain.

stench
stench

n. A bad smell.
The **stench** of rotting fish drove the investigators away from the dock.

strew
stro͞o

v. To scatter.
The wind **strewed** papers all over the yard.

vicinity
və sin´ ə tē

n. The nearby or surrounding area.
Is there a library in the **vicinity** of your home?

19A Finding Meanings

Choose two phrases to form a sentence that correctly uses a word from Word List 19. Write each sentence on the line provided.

1. (a) A haven is
   (b) a high wall to keep out enemies.
   (c) A breach is
   (d) an opening made by breaking through.

2. (a) vacate it on an agreed date.
   (b) To restore a building is to
   (c) To construct a building is to
   (d) bring it back to its original condition.

3. (a) To be in the vicinity is to be
   (b) aware of what is going on.
   (c) To be clammy is to be
   (d) close by.

4. (a) To elaborate is to
   (b) make no further effort.
   (c) provide more details.
   (d) To retaliate is to

5. (a) build it.
   (b) To furnish a room is to
   (c) To construct a room is to
   (d) put it to its intended use.

6. (a) Retaliation is
   (b) the act of breaking through.
   (c) Fragrance is
   (d) the returning of an injury.

7. (a) To furnish things
   (b) is to supply them.
   (c) is to take them apart.
   (d) To strew things

8. (a) is to hide it.
   (b) To install something
   (c) To repel something
   (d) is to fix it in place.

9. (a) A stench is
   (b) A haven is
   (c) a sneering remark.
   (d) a bad smell.

10. (a) A fragrance is
    (b) something that is put to regular use.
    (c) A repellent is
    (d) something that drives things away.

19B Just the Right Word

Improve each of the following sentences by crossing out the bold phrase and replacing it with a word (or a form of the word) from Word List 19.

1. Although only a few miles across, a neutron star can be as **heavy and contain as much matter** as the sun.

2. Rosa remembered the **pleasantly sweet smell** of the honeysuckle in her grandparents' garden.

3. You **failed to keep** my trust when you wouldn't stand up for me.

4. Prejudice of any kind is **so unpleasant that it is disgusting** to decent people.

5. A small inlet was the only **place of safety** for boats during the storm.

6. Kim had thought that a snake's skin would feel **cold and damp**, but it felt quite dry.

7. Many of these colonial houses have been **brought back to their original condition** by prominent builders.

8. Garbage was **spread about here and there** all over the sidewalk from the overturned trash cans.

9. The ad said you can **obtain all the furniture you need for** three rooms for under $1,000.

10. When she broke her promise to me, I **got back at her** by telling all her friends what she had done.

breach
clammy
construct
elaborate
fragrant
furnish
haven
install
massive
repel
restore
retaliate
stench
strew
vicinity

19C Applying Meanings

Circle the letter of each correct answer to the questions below. Each question has from one to four correct answers.

1. Which of the following might be **fragrant**?
   (a) garbage
   (b) a glass ornament
   (c) flowers
   (d) perfume

2. Which of the following could be **installed**?
   (a) new members
   (b) firewood
   (c) smoke detectors
   (d) a fireplace

3. Which of the following might have a **stench**?
   (a) roses
   (b) garbage
   (c) spoiled milk
   (d) rotten eggs

4. Which of the following could be **elaborate**?
   (a) a ceremony
   (b) a hoax
   (c) an exhibit
   (d) a gait

5. Which of the following can be **breached**?
   (a) a hoax
   (b) a wall
   (c) a contract
   (d) a friendship

6. Which of the following can be **restored**?
   (a) a fireplace
   (b) confidence
   (c) a painting
   (d) fatigue

7. Which of the following can be **repelled**?
   (a) an attack
   (b) a person
   (c) dogs
   (d) water

8. Which of the following can be **furnished**?
   (a) a room
   (b) an opportunity
   (c) supplies
   (d) anguish

19D Word Study

The prefix *re-* has two common meanings. It can mean "again" or it can mean "backward" or "back." Match each definition with the correct word chosen from the list. Write each word in the space provided.

restrain	relive	refill	reread
revise	recall	return	revive

1. To know again what one knew before ________________

2. To hold back by force or force of will ________________

3. To bring back to former state ________________

4. To fill again after being emptied ________________

5. To look over again and make changes ________________

6. To go over events in your mind ______________________

7. To bring back to a lively state ______________________

8. To go over material in a book again ______________________

19E Passage

Read the passage below; then complete the exercise that follows.

The Great Age of Castles

Castles seem magical places to those who have only read about them in fairy tales. The reality, however, was much different. Although they were homes to queens and kings and to great ladies and lords, we can tell from the castles that have survived that they were not pleasant places in which to live.

Their outside walls were made of **massive** blocks of stone and were up to twenty feet thick. Living inside such thick stone walls must have felt like living in a cave, for the rooms inside the castle were often **clammy**. Icy drafts blew through the narrow, glassless windows in winter, adding to the discomfort of the inhabitants. The **stench** from the animals kept inside the castle, as well as from the unwashed bodies of the people, would have been overpowering, especially during the heat of summer. **Fragrant** herbs were used to mask the smells; one of the servants' jobs was to **strew** them on the castle floors.

The great age of castle building was the seven-hundred-year period from around 800 to 1500. A castle built at the beginning of this period was a fairly simple wooden **construction** and has long since disappeared. One built later was made of stone and much more **elaborate**, with many private rooms, splendid **furnishings**, and a great hall where banquets were held and visitors were greeted and entertained.

The main reason for building a castle was to provide a sanctuary in times of danger, not only for those who made their homes inside its walls but also for those who lived in the **vicinity**. They could move inside the castle grounds if a hostile army approached. An attacking army had first to cross the moat, a wide, deep trench filled with water, which surrounded the castle. Then the attackers had to scale the high, outside walls on ladders or platforms. Those defending the castle could **retaliate** by shooting arrows at them or by dropping rocks or pouring boiling liquids on them. If the attackers were **repelled**, they might begin a siege, hoping to starve the defenders into surrendering. A siege could last for many months before one side or the other gave up.

When gunpowder came into use around 1500, cannons could **breach** even the thickest walls, and castles were no longer the **havens** they had once been. Many were abandoned and fell into ruin, but a number of them are still standing. In some cases their modern owners have **restored** them and made them more comfortable for today's occupants by **installing** modern plumbing and electricity. Many castles are open to the public as museums or luxury hotels. Today you can enjoy some of the bygone magic of castles by visiting castles in Germany, particularly along the Rhine River, and Great Britain.

breach
clammy
construct
elaborate
fragrant
furnish
haven
install
massive
repel
restore
retaliate
stench
strew
vicinity

Answer each of the following questions in the form of a sentence. If a question does not contain a vocabulary word from this lesson's word list, use one in your answer. Use each word only once. Questions and answers will then contain all fifteen words (or forms of the words).

1. What were the two main functions of castles?

2. What is the meaning of **construction** as it is used in the passage?

3. What would be the advantage of building castles near stone quarries?

4. Why are castles today more convenient and comfortable places to live in?

5. How did the building of castles evolve over the centuries?

6. Why would buying a ruined castle not appeal to a person of modest means?

7. How might a modern owner make a castle's rooms less **clammy**?

8. What **furnishings** might you find in the great hall of a castle?

9. What quality would have been valued in herbs grown in the castle gardens?

10. What difference would bathing regularly have made in the living conditions of the castle's inhabitants?

11. What use was made of the herbs grown in the castle gardens?

12. When might a castle have become overcrowded?

13. What is the meaning of **repelled** as it is used in the passage?

14. Name two ways that a castle's inhabitants could **retaliate** if attacked.

15. What is the meaning of **breach** as it is used in the passage?

FUN & FASCINATING FACTS

The adjective formed from **construct** is *constructive*, which means "helpful" or "useful." Its antonym is *destructive*, which means "damaging" or "unhelpful." *Constructive* criticism is intended to be helpful, but *destructive* criticism can be damaging to a person's self-confidence.

Mass is the noun from which the adjective **massive** is formed. Mass is the amount of matter in a body. It is separate from weight, which is a measure of how strongly gravity is pulling on the object. A spaceship in orbit has a great deal of mass but weighs nothing because gravity is not pulling it to Earth. Even a relatively small boulder contains a great deal of mass. A blimp, on the other hand, although it may be many times larger, contains very little mass; it is *enormous* but not *massive*.

Massive is also used in a figurative sense to describe something large in comparison with what is usual (a *massive* dose of a drug; a *massive* blood clot causing a stroke).

Lesson 20

Word List

Study the definitions of the words below; then do the exercises for the lesson.

bluster
blus´ tər

v. To talk in a loud and bullying manner.
"It's none of your business," he **blustered** when asked why he had stolen the money.
n. Loud, boastful or threatening talk or commotion.
They can talk tough, but their **bluster** doesn't scare me.
blustering *adj.* Blowing loudly and violently.
The **blustering** winds buffeted the ferry as it crossed the lake.

council
koun´ səl

n. A group of people who meet to decide or plan something, give advice, or make laws.
Members of the town **council** are elected for a two-year term.

dwell
dwel

v. 1. To live or reside.
How long did you **dwell** in the house where you were born?
2. To keep thinking about.
It does no good to **dwell** on past mistakes.
dwelling *n.* A house or home.
The only difference between one **dwelling** and the next was the color of the doors and shutters.

exterminate
ek stur´ mi nāt

v. To kill or destroy completely.
It can be difficult to **exterminate** mistletoe from oak trees.

fee
fē

n. A fixed sum of money charged.
The admission **fee** for the art museum is five dollars.

garment
gär´ mənt

n. Any piece of clothing.
These delicate **garments** should be washed by hand.

infest
in fest´

v. To overrun in a way that causes harm or annoyance.
Drastic measures are needed to deal with the drug dealers who **infest** the city.

insist
in sist´

v. To take a stand and hold firmly to it.
The owners **insist** that the tenants vacate the property by the end of the month.
insistent *adj.* (in sis´ tənt) Unyielding; firm.
The bird watcher was **insistent** that everyone visit the bird sanctuary.

paltry
pôl´ trē

adj. Very small and worthless; hardly worth considering.
Five dollars may seem a **paltry** sum today, but in 1914 it was a day's wage for an automobile worker.

peculiar
pi kyōōl´ yər

adj. 1. Odd; strange.
It seems **peculiar** that such a frugal person would give everyone extravagant gifts.
2. Limited to a person, country, group, or thing.
Koalas are **peculiar** to Australia.

rash
rash

n. 1. A breaking out of red spots on the skin.
This ointment will soothe the baby's **rash**.
2. A series of outbreaks.
A **rash** of burglaries disturbed the area right after Labor Day.
adj. Too hasty or reckless.
I regretted the **rash** statements I made while I was angry.

revenge
rē venj´

n. 1. The desire to return harm for harm done.
Revenge for past wrongs was the only thing on their minds.
2. The act of paying back wrong done.
"I'll have my **revenge**," said the victim of the hoax.
v. To get even for a wrong done; to retaliate.
The Sheriff of Nottingham swore to **revenge** the raids made by Robin Hood.

rodent
rōd´ nt

n. An animal with sharp teeth for gnawing.
Small **rodents** such as gerbils and hamsters are popular pets.
adj. Of or relating to rodents.
The **rodent** droppings in the attic were a sign of mice.

swarm
swôrm

v. To move in large numbers.
Soccer fans **swarmed** into the stadium for the final game of the series.
n. A large, moving crowd or mass.
The bees emerged from the hive in a dense **swarm**.

vat
vat

n. A large container such as a tub or barrel used for holding liquids.
Olive oil is stored in these large **vats**.

bluster
council
dwell
exterminate
fee
garment
infest
insist
paltry
peculiar
rash
revenge
rodent
swarm
vat

20A Finding Meanings

Choose two phrases to form a sentence that correctly uses a word from Word List 20. Write each sentence on the line provided.

1. (a) a small and worthless amount.
   (b) A vat is
   (c) a series of outbreaks.
   (d) A rash is

2. (a) A dwelling is
   (b) a group of people who meet to plan something.
   (c) A council is
   (d) a large tub for holding liquids.

3. (a) threatening or boastful talk.
   (b) Bluster is
   (c) anything that seems strange or unusual.
   (d) Revenge is

4. (a) A garment is
   (b) anything of little or no value.
   (c) A swarm is
   (d) an article of clothing.

5. (a) To revenge something is
   (b) To insist on something is
   (c) to get even for it.
   (d) to refuse to worry about it.

6. (a) to take a stand against it.
   (b) To exterminate something is
   (c) to get rid of it by destroying it.
   (d) To infest something is

7. (a) refuse to change one's mind.
   (b) be unable to make up one's mind.
   (c) To be peculiar is to
   (d) To be insistent is to

8. (a) A swarm is
   (b) a large, moving crowd.
   (c) an article of clothing.
   (d) A fee is

9. (a) A dwelling is
   (b) a charge made for a service.
   (c) a container for liquids.
   (d) A vat is

20B Just the Right Word

Improve each of the following sentences by crossing out the bold phrase and replacing it with a word (or a form of the word) from Word List 20.

1. A(n) **outbreak of red spots on the skin** usually is the first sign of chicken pox.

2. The wind started to **blow wildly and cause all kinds of damage** as the hurricane gathered strength.

3. I was **not willing to change my mind about my demand** that she give me the car keys.

4. Rats or other **animals with sharp front teeth used for gnawing** had chewed through the wall.

5. It's a good idea to lay out all one's **articles of clothing** before starting to pack one's suitcase.

6. This powder will **get rid of all** the fleas in your house.

7. The bald eagle is **a creature that is native only** to North America.

8. Francis Bacon tells us that **the desire to return harm for harm done** is a kind of wild justice.

9. Ten dollars seems a **small and almost worthless** prize for the winner of the chess match.

10. The **price of admission** for students is half the regular rate.

11. The woodwork is **suffering damage because it is overrun** with termites.

12. It does no good to **keep your mind only** on failures of the past.

20C Applying Meanings

Circle the letter of each correct answer to the questions below. Each question has from one to four correct answers.

bluster
council
dwell
exterminate
fee
garment
infest
insist
paltry
peculiar
rash
revenge
rodent
swarm
vat

1. For which of the following might you pay a **fee**?
   (a) an examination by a doctor
   (b) an expedition to the Arctic
   (c) a trip to the local supermarket
   (d) a round of miniature golf

2. Which of the following is a **dwelling**?
   (a) a garage
   (b) a cabin
   (c) a cottage
   (d) a church

3. Which of the following might a person want **exterminated**?
   (a) fleas
   (b) cockroaches
   (c) rats
   (d) ants

4. Which of the following might members of a **council** do?
   (a) pass laws
   (b) meet regularly
   (c) offer advice
   (d) run for reelection

5. Which of the following are **rodents**?
   (a) cats
   (b) mice
   (c) squirrels
   (d) frogs

6. Which of the following might **bluster**?
   (a) an arrogant speaker
   (b) a storm
   (c) a timid customer
   (d) a cordial host

7. Which of the following might seem **peculiar**?
   (a) a rich person begging in the street
   (b) a pet lobster
   (c) a person who doesn't eat meat
   (d) a mouse chasing a cat

8. Which of the following can **swarm**?
   (a) bees
   (b) trees
   (c) people
   (d) years

20D Word Study

Select the pair of words that most nearly expresses the relationship of the pair of words in capital letters. Circle the letter in front of the pair you choose.

1. FRAGRANT : SMELL ::
   (a) sweet : sugar
   (b) sour : lemon
   (c) melodious : sound
   (d) bitter : taste

2. MOBILE : STATIONARY ::
   (a) versatile : talented
   (b) massive: colossal
   (c) elated : exhilarated
   (d) loyal : treacherous

3. STERN : BOAT ::
   (a) gait : walk
   (b) scale : map
   (c) tail : dog
   (d) ship : sail

4. LOOM : WEAVE ::
   (a) song : compose
   (b) coat : apparel
   (c) ferry : transport
   (d) cloth : cotton

5. PLACID : HECTIC ::
   (a) warm : hot
   (b) benevolent : wicked
   (c) cool : cold
   (d) exhausted : fatigued

6. JACKET : GARMENT ::
   (a) wool : silk
   (b) hammer : tool
   (c) shoe : leather
   (d) sweater : skirt

7. SWARM : BEES ::
   (a) hive : honey
   (b) wool : sheep
   (c) scale : fish
   (d) herd : cattle

8. ANTICIPATE : FUTURE ::
   (a) remember : past
   (b) solve : problem
   (c) forget : time
   (d) answer : question

9. HOUSE : DWELLING ::

(a) table : chair
(b) village : city
(c) chimney : roof
(d) haven : sanctuary

10. MINUTE : MICROSCOPE ::

(a) warm : thermometer
(b) distant : telescope
(c) comfortable : armchair
(d) fast : rocket

20E Passage

Read the passage below; then complete the exercise that follows.

The Pied Piper of Hamelin

Rats!
They fought the dogs, and killed the cats,
And bit the babies in the cradles,
And ate the cheeses out of the **vats**,
And licked the soup from the cooks' own ladles. . .*

There was no doubt that the people of Hamelin had a very serious problem. Their town was **infested** with rats, and the furry, beady-eyed **rodents** had grown so bold that they had invaded the people's cellars, their kitchens, and even their bedrooms. There wasn't a **dwelling** in the town that wasn't teeming with rats. The people threatened to run the mayor out of town unless he did something about the problem. The mayor promised to get rid of the rats: he vowed to **exterminate** every rat in town; he **blustered** that not a rat would be left alive. But what could he do? Nothing except meet with his **council** to discuss ways of solving the problem. And the truth was that neither he nor anyone else had the faintest idea what to do.

Suddenly a man dressed in a most **peculiar** fashion appeared at the meeting. His quaint **garments** drew stares and comments from the townspeople.

His queer long coat from heel to head
Was half of yellow and half of red.

The stranger in the pied coat promised to rid the town of its rats by luring them away with the music from his pipe for a **fee** of one thousand guilders. The mayor was overjoyed and replied that that was too **paltry** a sum for performing such a task. He promised to pay fifty thousand guilders!

Everyone followed as the Pied Piper stepped into the street. He raised his pipe to his lips and began to play. Over the sound of the music a strange noise could be heard.

And the muttering grew to a grumbling;
And the grumbling grew to a mighty rumbling;
And out of the houses the rats came tumbling.

Rats **swarmed** into the streets and followed the Pied Piper as he led them out of town. When they came to the river Weser, the rats plunged in and perished.

bluster
council
dwell
exterminate
fee
garment
infest
insist
paltry
peculiar
rash
revenge
rodent
swarm
vat

* The quotations in rhyme are taken from Robert Browning's poem "The Pied Piper of Hamelin," a fanciful story about a town in Germany.

The people of Hamelin were most grateful to the Pied Piper and rang every bell in town to celebrate, but the mayor was having second thoughts. He felt that he had been **rash** to offer fifty thousand guilders. He now thought a mere fifty guilders would be enough! When the Pied Piper **insisted** on being paid in full, the mayor laughed in his face.

> You threaten us, fellow? Do your worst,
> Blow your pipe there till you burst!

As his **revenge**, the Pied Piper led away the village's children, who were never seen again.

Answer each of the following questions in the form of a sentence. If a question does not contain a vocabulary word from this lesson's word list, use one in your answer. Use each word only once. Questions and answers will then contain all fifteen words (or forms of the words).

1. Why were the inhabitants of Hamelin probably afraid to enter their homes?

2. Was any part of the town free of rats?

3. What was the mayor's problem in dealing with the town's **rodent** problem?

4. Vats usually hold liquids. Why do you think the poet says the cheese was in **vats**?

5. Where did the Pied Piper make his offer to get rid of the rats?

6. Why did the Pied Piper's **garments** arouse so much interest among the townspeople?

7. How much did the Pied Piper say he would charge for getting rid of the rats?

8. What did the mayor think of the amount of money the Pied Piper requested?

9. Why was it **rash** of the mayor to offer 50,000 guilders to the Pied Piper?

10. What did the astonished townspeople see when the Pied Piper began to play?

11. How did the Pied Piper **exterminate** the rats?

12. How did the mayor behave when the Pied Piper rejected the fifty guilders?

13. What is the meaning of **peculiar** as it is used in the passage?

14. Why do you think the Pied Piper **insisted** on being paid in full?

15. In what way does the passage end on a sinister note?

FUN & FASCINATING FACTS

Low German was the language spoken in northern Germany for several centuries up to around 1500. The word for a rag in that language is *palte*, and the adjective *paltrig* means "ragged."

Paltrig passed into English as our word **paltry**. Something that is ragged is of very little value, so it is easy to see how *paltry* came to mean "of little value" or "worthless."

Avenge and **revenge** are similar in meaning. A person can both *avenge* a wrong and revenge a wrong. There is a difference that should be noted, however.

Avenge suggests striking back at a wrongdoer in order to obtain justice. Hamlet, in the play of the same name, is called upon to *avenge* his father's murder by killing his uncle, who had committed the crime. Hamlet takes no satisfaction from his action, which he feels has been forced upon him.

Revenge carries the suggestion of striking back at a wrongdoer for the personal satisfaction it brings. Note that *revenge* is both a verb and a noun. *Avenge* is a verb only.

A **council** is a group of people that meets to decide or plan something, give advice, or make laws. A town council may be the ruling body of a town. A president may appoint a council to look into an issue and offer advice. Students may elect a students' council to govern their affairs. People who are members of a council are called *councillors*.

Counsel is advice or opinion. When one is faced with seemingly unsolvable problems, it may be advisable to seek counsel. A person who gives counsel as a profession is called a *counselor*.

Review for Lessons 17–20

Hidden Message In the boxes provided, write the words from Lessons 17 through 20 that are missing in each of the sentences below. The number following each sentence gives the word list from which the missing word is taken. When the exercise is finished, the shaded boxes should spell out some well-known words from the pen of Sir Walter Scott, the Scottish novelist and poet.

1. The _____ started over a ban on rock groups. (18)

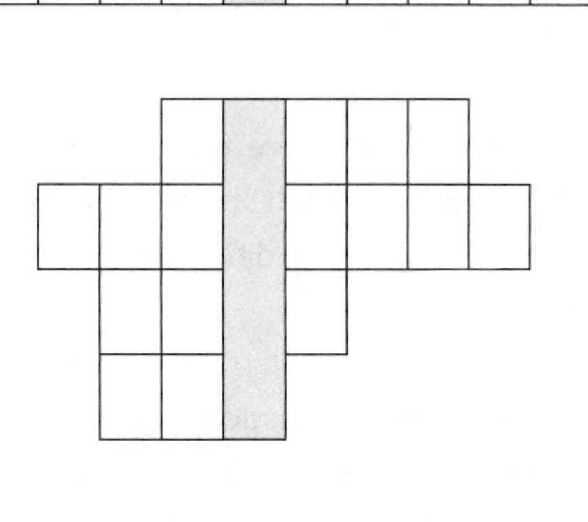

2. Shoppers _____ into the malls every December. (20)
3. Her efforts to impress people seemed _____ . (17)
4. Their story of winning a million dollars was a _____ . (18)
5. The peasants emptied the _____ that held the yellow dye. (20)

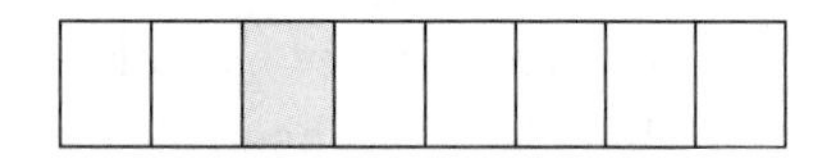

6. Lavender is a delightfully _____ herb. (19)

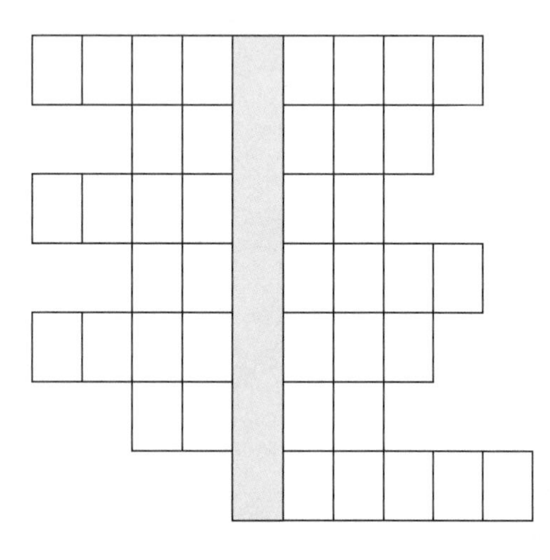

7. Be _____ if something sounds too good to be true. (18)
8. The child's forehead became _____ because of a fever. (19)
9. The scoundrel swore to take _____ on the investigator who tried to thwart him. (20)
10. The death of their pet caused them great _____ . (18)
11. Bald eagles are _____ to North America. (20)
12. The villagers _____ in simple huts built of pine logs. (20)
13. _____ from the explosion was scattered widely. (17)

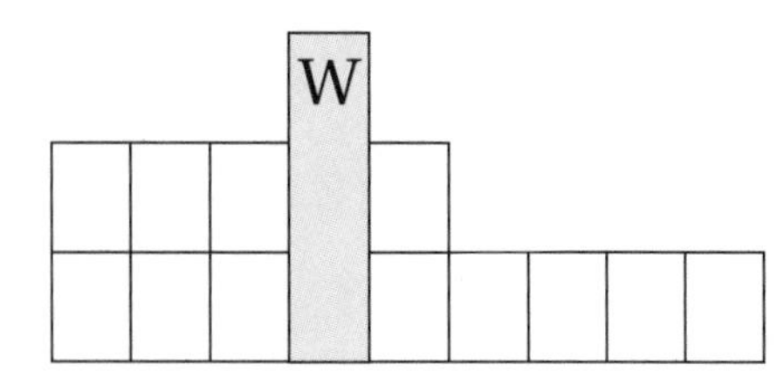

14. The island is a _____ of peace in a troubled world. (19)
15. The council would like you to _____ on your outline for the concert. (19)

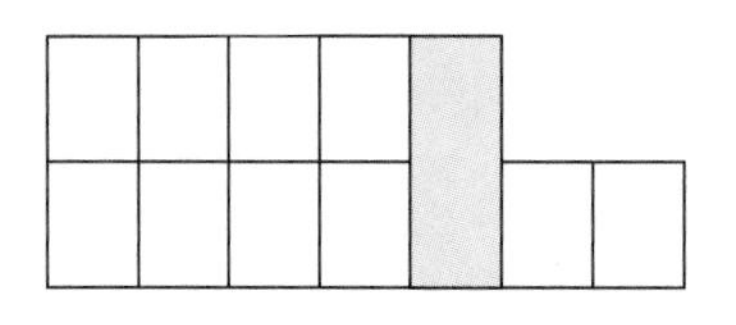

16. Don't _____ your dirty clothes all over the floor. (19)
17. The principal will _____ those students for doing such a fine job. (18)

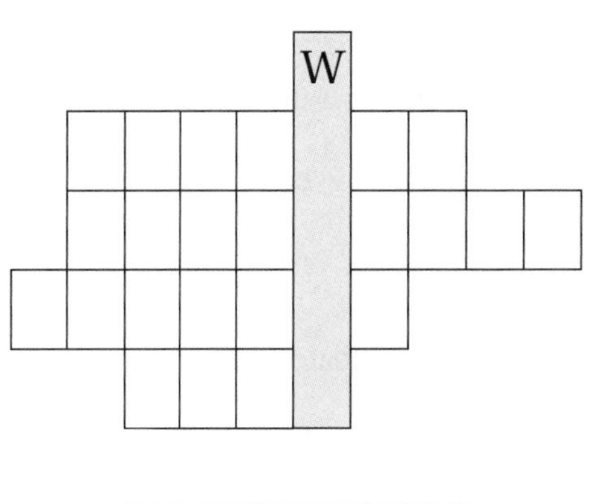

18. This _____ will last a long time if washed by hand. (20)
19. The locket held a _____ portrait of her mother. (17)
20. A _____ boulder that had rolled onto the road was blocking our way and couldn't be moved. (19)
21. Blood began to _____ from the cut on my hand. (17)

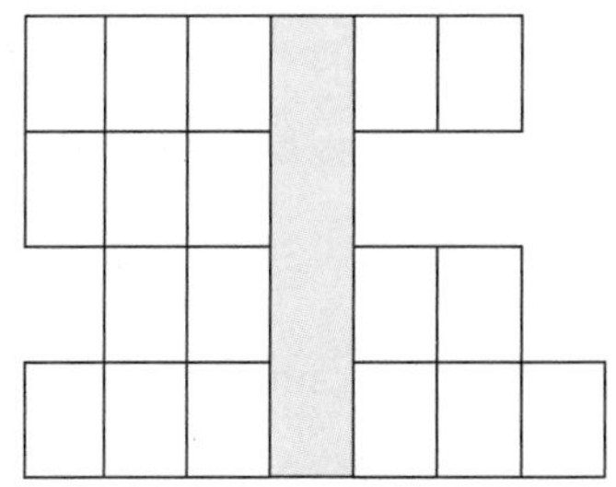

22. The double-parked cars left no _____ for the bus to pass. (17)
23. The recent _____ of burglaries has the residents worried. (20)
24. Their _____ for knowledge about their ancestors led them abroad. (17)
25. Please _____ them with the information they request. (19)

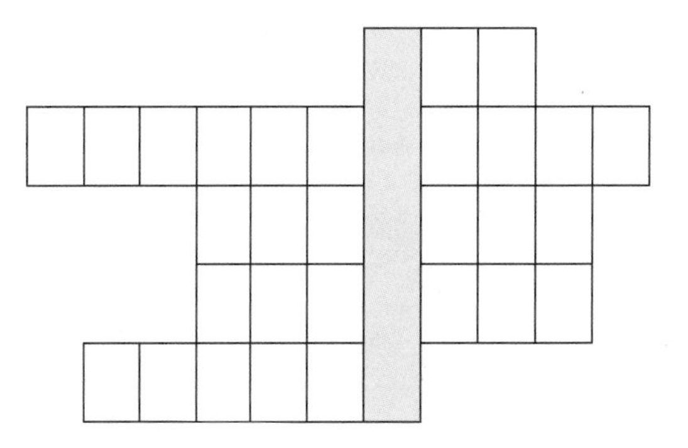

26. The doctor's _____ was eighty dollars. (20)
27. _____ tests will indicate whether more extensive tests are needed. (17)
28. The salt air will soon _____ the metal. (17)
29. Insecure people sometimes _____ to hide their fears. (20)
30. My parents _____ that I do my homework before watching television. (20)

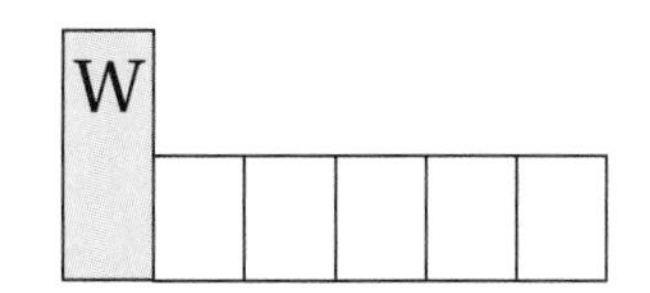

31. The fan's letters to the movie star failed to _____ a reply. (18)

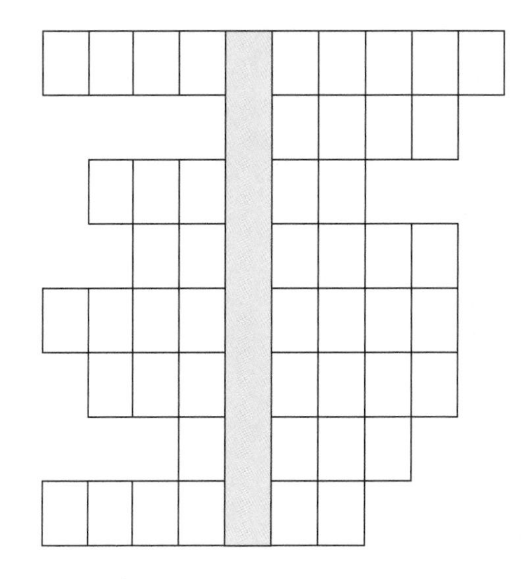

32. The assembler will expertly _____ the controls. (18)
33. The fabric this tent is made of will _____ water. (19)
34. An honest person will not _____ an agreement. (19)
35. There was not time to _____ all my adventures. (18)
36. It took two years to _____ the new hospital wing. (19)
37. The lost dog was last seen in the _____ of the bus station. (19)
38. The only way to make these pots shine is to _____ them. (17)
39. Three jurors say they will _____ from the majority vote. (18)

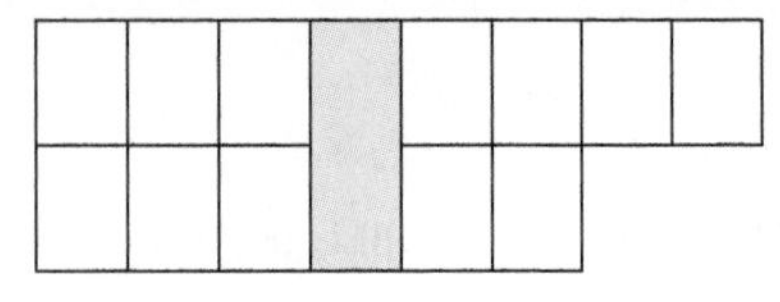

40. Those on a diet must _____ themselves at mealtimes. (17)

41. I had never been _____ until my trip to Africa. (18)

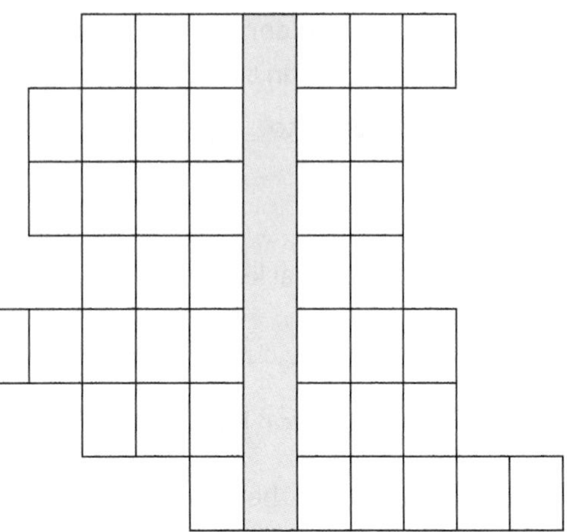

42. The negotiator was given a _____ welcome by the opposing sides. (18)

43. We made an _____ attempt to find the owner. (18)

44. The town _____ has the power to raise taxes. (20)

45. Porcupines belong to the _____ family. (20)

46. He didn't _____ when angered because of his self-control. (19)

47. Were the survivors able to _____ anything from the fire? (17)

48. The painting may be _____ , but the experts seem skeptical. (18)

Review for Lessons 17–20

Crossword Puzzle Solve the crossword puzzle below by studying the clues and filling in the answer boxes. Clues followed by a number are definitions of words in Lessons 17 through 20. The number gives the word list in which the answer to the clue appears.

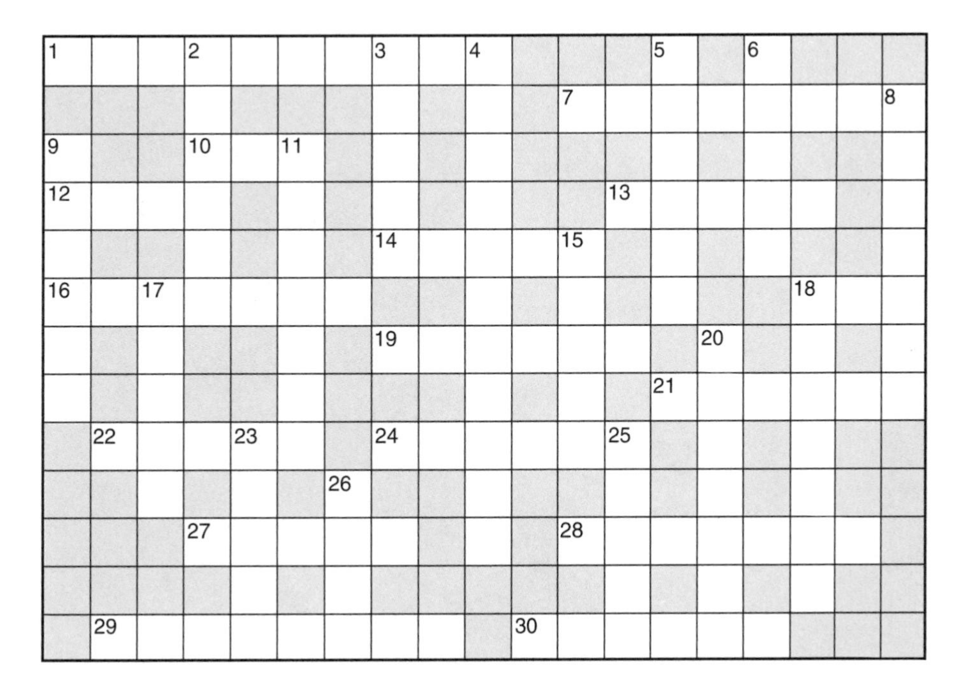

Clues Across

1. To excite or stimulate (18)
7. Causing feelings of pity or sorrow (17)
10. A payment for a service performed (20)
12. To leak out slowly (17)
13. The beginning or start (17)
14. To scatter (19)
16. To fix in position; to set up (19)
18. A large container for liquids (20)
19. To draw out or to cause (18)
21. Cold and damp (19)
22. A hunt or search for something precious (17)
24. Happy and excited (17)
27. A place of safety (19)
28. To bring back to the original condition (19)
29. To begin; to make a start (18)
30. Very small in amount; worthless (20)

Clues Down

2. To overrun in a way that harms or bothers (20)
3. A book of maps
4. To kill or destroy completely (20)
5. A bad or offensive smell (19)
6. To drive back or fight off (19)
8. Opposite of *town*
9. Able to move freely (17)
11. To make full use of (17)
15. Red, ________ , and blue
17. To search thoroughly (17)
18. Count Dracula, for example
20. To talk loudly and boastfully (20)
23. To move in large numbers (20)
25. To live or reside (20)
26. An abbreviation for *Pennsylvania*